BEHIND THE RODS

To Andrew
have a best wishes

Jenny

March 2019

BEHIND
the
RODS

TALES OF A
WITCH AND A WIZARD

Jenny Vardy

Matador
9 Priory Business Park,
Wistow Road, Kibworth Beauchamp,
Leicestershire, LE8 0RX
Tel: 0116 279 2299
Email: books@troubador.co.uk
Web: www.troubador.co.uk/matador
Twitter: @matadorbooks

ISBN 978 1789017 991

British Library Cataloguing in Publication Data.
A catalogue record for this book is available from the British Library.

Printed and bound in Great Britain by 4edge Limited
Typeset in 11pt Adobe Garamond Pro by Troubador Publishing Ltd, Leicester, UK

Matador is an imprint of Troubador Publishing Ltd

We dedicate this book to all those who have generously allowed us to share their stories with you, our readers. The book is scattered with some very personal experiences. The purpose of relating these encounters is important in demonstrating the range and scope of the diviners' powers and to show how their skills might be used beneficially. In these cases, every care has been taken to conceal identity and preserve privacy. In the most sensitive cases the experiences have been fictionalised, leaving only the skeleton of the dowsers' activities. But we know you, and we thank you sincerely.

We also owe an enormous thanks to those who have shown enthusiasm for our work and have trudged many miles with us, questioning their rods and reporting their results. Without you there would be no book.

– CONTENTS –

– INTRODUCTION –

*"True scepticism does not begin by being anti-
anything. The process of open consideration and
examination (i.e. research) will ultimately establish
whether something exists or not".*

Ingo Swann

As you stroll through these pages, I, an interested observer
and narrator, will lead you on a journey – an odyssey that will
take you across continents and across time. In the company
of two extra-ordinary companions, you will pass from the
mechanical and mundane to the mystical and magical.

They will share with you experiences that many of you
would have thought impossible.

Others have written weighty, well-researched, scientific
or historical tomes, that have dealt in depth with a variety
of aspects mentioned here. Some have dwelt on the ancient
links that have been made with black magic and the occult,
while others have stressed the practical and scientific aspects
of this art or skill. Records of dowsers at work appeared in
wood cuts as early as the sixteenth century. While the fear of

links with black magic persists in some quarters even today, as early as the 1800s one English local government bravely faced such accusations and gave official recognition to the practice of dowsing for water.

'In 1927 the London Times ran a leading article entitled "Dowsers and Doubters", which prompted a flood of letters both for and against – those who had used the skill for years and those who condemned it as a con or worse, dabbling in black magic'. Ref: 'Mystery Gift of Dowsing' by Patrick Coyne. Weekend Angus Feb 3rd 2018.

This book does not aim to be an academic treatise and yet, while it is largely anecdotal, certain disciplines of research have not been neglected, and where facts are quoted they are verifiable.

You will travel back into the realms of pre-history and follow links to the present day and even speculative projections to the future.

Together we aim to entertain you, but also provide you with food for thought. We will not preach, nor teach, but merely report events and share our thoughts. What you make of it all is up to you, but our hope is that when you reach the last page you will be full of wonder at the world around you; that you will be changed, being more aware and challenged, and that you will be left with a deep-seated need to search for further knowledge and enlightenment.

part one

A Trip Through the Ages

Millions of years ago, before the age of man, wild animals freely roamed the earth. Not all times and places were hospitable, and animals fought for survival. In order to do so they developed 'life skills'. The efficiency of these skills determined their success. This was the basis of Darwin's Theory of the 'Survival of the Fittest'. In other words, those animals that were most successful were those who had adapted best to their environment and had developed skills that would enable them to survive.

One of the most basic needs of all animals is water and this was not always universally abundant. Only animals that developed an infallible ability to detect the presence of water over, often, great distances were likely to survive and so protect their species. Even today we know that elephants in the wild will travel many tedious miles and eventually, unerringly, dig deep into the ground to find their precious drink.

For as long as animal behaviour has been observed, and later recorded, it has been known that many birds and animals follow a variety of set 'genetic' patterns which aim to increase their success and the continuation of their species.

It is true that some creatures, like the dinosaurs, either through some cataclysmic event like an Ice Age or a failure to adapt adequately to their environment, became extinct, but they are the minority. Most animals show an incredible ability to use nature to their advantage.

Many birds and even butterflies migrate incredible distances to ensure congenial environments for feeding and breeding. Some, like the North American humming birds, will start their annual migration with an outstanding sense of timing and will usually leave their summer abode within a five-day window each year, returning in the early summer within a similar time span. Like so many others, they will follow the same route over thousands of miles and will return to the same spots every year.

Similarly, the migration of eels to the Sargasso Sea is legendary, also the spawning of salmon in the same rivers.

Why they do this is not in question – they are travelling to an environment that is historically known to be more suited to their needs in that season.

How they do it is definitely the subject of speculative research. Many theories have been advanced including built-in genetic pathways, genetic memory, parental modelling, stellar direction-finding, sea currents and more. All these may certainly play a part, but we do not believe that these hold the final answer.

An elephant, indeed any animal, who cannot find water will die, ipso facto, those who survive have the ability to find water. They have a sensitivity to water that transcends great distances and depths. In our terms they are 'water diviners'.

One popular theory of bird migration propounded by science is that migratory routes are tracked by the stars, but birds continue their long and arduous flights by day and on cloudy nights when no stars are visible.

Fish and eel migration is thought to be directed by sea currents but these are often disturbed and disrupted by violent storms and yet the migration route is left unimpaired.

It is our belief that the final key to the accuracy of animal navigation, of all types, is the vast spherical network of electromagnetic energy that forms a tight grid across our globe. The ability to perceive and use this grid is a life-skill for all animals. It was inherent in the skills of early man, his only means of survival, but gradually as life became more 'civilised' it was a skill on which he was less dependent, and his sensitivity atrophied. It was a classic case of 'use it or lose it'.

As our dowsers' awareness of our own sensitivity grew, its strength amazed them and it has been an increasing revelation to discover that, in fact, this skill has lain dormant in most people over thousands of years and it is there just awaiting its awakening.

Early Man

When Man arrived on earth, he too was in competition with the animals for the basic necessities of life, food and water. In primitive times homo-sapiens would have had the sensitivity to find water even when it was hidden beneath the ground. He would not have needed a dowsing tool as many dowsers need to use today, as his very body would have had that sensitivity.

It is believed that he also had a deep-seated sensitivity to the natural electromagnetic lines that encircle the earth and he would, perhaps, even subconsciously, use this ability to follow a fixed path and find directions, as accurately as with modern electronic satellite navigation. There is certainly evidence that ancient tribes like the San in South Africa have incredibly well-developed senses to a variety of stimuli unseen, unheard, unfelt by others, and can track a prey with uncanny accuracy over many miles.

We also have written evidence from very early times that there were also, perhaps only a few, exceptional people, whose sensitivity was far beyond that of the average person. If we believe that the Old Testament is the ultimate record of early Man's response to happenings that had been witnessed, in some cases, many years earlier, and passed through generations by family and folklore, to be finally written down, we may like to look more closely at some of these events in the light of our present knowledge and experience. Many historical characters and events recorded in these writings have been verified by numerous other documents. Research over the years has been both extensive and intensive. Kings, leaders and battles have been confirmed but it is not these that interest us in this context. We are concerned with the extra-ordinary, the experiences and recordings that cannot easily and obviously be explained. As Man's understanding was limited by his knowledge and experience at the time, the recorder, inevitably, imparted his own interpretation. Until the turn of the 16th century and the scientific work of the mathematician and astronomer, Copernicus, Man had believed the earth to be the centre of the Universe. He believed this was logical as he clearly saw the sun rise in the east in the morning and set in the west every day and he was standing on the earth and was not moving and so 'obviously' it was the sun that was moving around the earth. Although Aristarchus of Samos had proposed a heliocentric theory some 18 centuries earlier he had been scorned and ignored. Similarly, because Man and animals were standing upright on the earth and they could see to the far horizon they believed the earth was clearly flat. No-one to their limited knowledge had fallen off the edge and until the work of Isaac Newton and the revelation of 'magic' of gravity, Man had no reason to believe differently. Many strange and unexplained phenomena such as floods, tsunamis and rainbows would usually be referred to as an 'act of God', a 'blessing from God', a 'punishment from God' or a 'miracle'.

However, it is possible that something quite different was being witnessed and nature itself holds the keys to the understanding of these happenings.

When Moses tapped the rock at the place now called Wadi Musa, in Jordan, and the life-giving water poured freely, surely, he was acting as a modern-day dowser. He had led his people to a place where his dowser's instinct had indicated the presence of a natural spring.

We understand that Moses was a leader of his people in spiritual, as well as temporal, matters and it is therefore entirely possible that he, in fact, held the spiritual and mystic gifts of a Shaman, able to detect the earth energy, of which others were unaware. He 'talked' to God.

(Today, many seeking spiritual guidance will turn to those who have the gifts of a Shaman. These are mystic leaders who are said to treat the ailments of the body by first mending the soul. In this way they restore a natural balance between body and spirit producing a whole. They can act as intermediaries between human and spiritual worlds, and by their ability to enter other worlds they can bring messages and advice.

But, it is also true that similar gifts can be used for evil as well as good and in some communities, those known to have these powers are feared and shunned. This is certainly seen in primitive tribes where the equivalent leader and holder of power is the witch doctor. The people will turn to him for healing and blessing, but he is also renowned for his dreaded curses. Voodoo is also an extension of this. There is no doubt of these powers, but it is believed that in some cases autosuggestion and the 'self-fulfilling prophecy' can play a large part in the eventual outcomes.)

The 'miraculous burning bush' at St Catherine's Monastery in the Sinai desert was not consumed by fire and yet, according to the Old Testament, flames were seen leaping from it. No purpose is given for this, apparently, pointless 'miracle'. A possible theory is that the location is a point of extremely strong earth energy and the bush grew vigorously on an energy-rich portal. Just as energy, in various forms, can be picked up on some sensitive cameras – orbs, sprites and flashes – so there are specially gifted people who can 'see' this energy. Perhaps the individual who first witnessed this 'burning bush' was one such person and related his experience with this description, to be re-told and later recorded for posterity. The observation of energy auras is not unique and could well be an explanation of the strange phenomenon. The purpose of relating these reports is not to deny that the events took place but more to acknowledge them and demystify them.

It is generally accepted that some people, throughout history, have possessed extra-ordinary power to detect various forms of natural energy. It is also believed that all individuals are surrounded by an energy field that manifests aspects of their personality and their 'spirit'. This is called their 'aura'. While it is a gift not given to many, there are those today who can actually 'see' the auras surrounding others. The question arises whether this vision of auras was the origin of the 'haloes' portrayed around holy people of the past.

From earliest civilisations, and not least in the writings of the Church, there have been stories of people seeing visions. These have usually been associated with religious experiences, but one can also speculate that these sightings were of a similar origin to the appearance of ghosts. There have been many theories propounded on two of the best-known, more recent visions related to members of the Catholic Church. In 1858, Bernadette Soubirous, a peasant girl living in the Pyrenees near Nevers, reported no less than 18 separate visions of a young girl she later referred to as the Immaculate Conception. She was a sickly, uneducated girl, who spoke only the local Catalan patois, and yet she was able to relate details of her visions which in some cases lasted for nearly an hour. Although she was often in the company of her sister and a friend, neither of them saw the visions. During the visitations Bernadette maintained that she had received messages and requests from the Virgin Mary in response to which, eventually, a shrine and then a church was built at Lourdes, which now draws as many as five million pilgrims a year. Most come seeking cures from the reputed 'health-giving' waters, and in truth some have been cured, to the medical bafflement of their physicians.

The other well-known example was the message brought to the three Portuguese shepherd children at Fatima in 1917. Again it was the Virgin Mary who appeared, and this time with apocalyptic and prophetic messages. On this occasion all three children reported to have seen the vision. Over the years there has been considerable controversy outside and within the Church as to the meaning of the three messages. It was many years before Lucia, the eldest of the children, released any information about the messages. Eventually, she did disclose that the 'Lady' had told her that the First World War would soon end. However, the second message warned of another major war. Although Lucia was ordered by the Bishop to reveal the content of the third message, she did so only reluctantly on her death bed. The Church then chose to keep it secret until 2000 when the Pope did make a version of it public. However, it was not straightforward and the true meaning of the message has remained obscure and subject to a variety of interpretation.

These, of course, are only two of the very many stories, through the course of time, of visions, sightings, apparitions, some with messages some just appearances, over which people muse. Some will accept them without question, while others will discard them as complete fakes, some will consider them as the images of an over-active mind, while others will look for other explanations.

However, medical science has now revealed that the chemical imbalances that produces conditions like schizophrenia can cause the sufferer to experience very clear visions and also 'out-of-body' experiences.

It is also well known that people on hallucinatory drugs have very real visions when their sensory responses to their environment are exceptionally heightened.

However, neither of these conditions could account for visions that bring quite accurate and profound prophesies to young, uneducated minds.

The New Testament abounds with stories of miraculous cures and the 'laying-on of hands' but this was not a practice confined to that era. Psychic and Pranic healing is by no means a lost gift and increasing numbers of people, disillusioned with modern medical practice, with its emphasis on synthetic pharmaceutical drugs, are turning again to the ancient arts of herbs and 'energy balance' to seek a cure.

Middle Ages

Mediaeval times saw a proliferation of religions and the intensification of religious fervour. Certainly, the Christian Church became very powerful and ruled its followers with a doctrine of fear. It was undoubtedly ruthless in subduing any foreseen threat to its dogma, authority and power. Those gifted with the ability to 'faith heal' or communicate with spirits, were seen as a challenge to the omnipotence of God and were branded as witches and faced the horror of the 'ducking stool' or the terror of 'burning at the stake'. Yet witches prevailed and tales of magic abounded. The legends of Arthur and his Knights were intricately intertwined with the witchcraft of Merlin and Morgana.

It was also the age of alchemy when a legitimate search for knowledge mingled imperceptible with magic and the occult. The alchemists' obsession with finding a way to turn base metals into gold led to many inadvertent scientific discoveries, but it would not be until Mendeleef, Lothar Meyer and a number of other gifted and intuitive researchers, along with the invention of spectrometry, in the mid-19th century that it was realised that each element was distinctive and, while it may combine with other elements and so lose its identity in the compound, it was not possible to change one element into another by chemical means. Meanwhile, throughout the interim ages the practice of alchemy was shrouded in mystery and suspicion.

It was due to the suppressive actions of the Church that the psychic arts were forced into secrecy. Despite this, even factions within the Church itself were seeing the value of these gifts for their own advantage. The Knights Templar were a group who left considerable evidence around the world of their understanding of, and proficiency in, the occult. Many learned scholars have studied Templar signs in an attempt to interpret them and links have been made with Masonic rites and even the inexplicably intricate designs of crop circles.

There is evidence that from the time Man started to build dwellings there were people who understood natural earth energy and could identify what we now call 'ley lines'. Even Stone Age settlements are sited so that their 'special' places, those of worship or sacrifice, are located on powerful energy lines.

Distinctive structures classed as 'Wonders of the World', like Stonehenge and the Pyramids, lie directly on ley lines.

The Middle Ages was a time when vast wealth was being spent on building churches and huge cathedrals throughout the Christian world. This was not unique as the world of Islam had started building its vast mosques to the glory of Allah, every city in Europe had its synagogue, and the skylines in Far Eastern cities were broken with the towering domes and turrets of Hindu and Buddhist shrines and temples. Every one of these edifices, whatever its age, or country, has been found to rest on a natural 'earth energy line' or 'ley line'.

We now know that this is also true of all important buildings used for education and justice. What we do not know is how the original builders knew and how much they understood. We also do not know if communal worship in a building on a positive ley line increases the positive energy at that place.

Christ is reported to have said, "For where two or three are gathered together in my name, there am I in the midst of them" (Matthew 18:20). Was this perhaps an acknowledgement of the spiritual power of mass invocation? Is this the real power of 'all-night vigils'?

Wiltshire has long been accepted as an area of high spiritual presence. It has been historically, and for some, mythically, associated with Joseph of Arimathea, the Holy Grail and the mysterious legends of the various 'henges'. For years, it has been the main area in the United Kingdom for crop circles, those intricate patterns, appearing in corn fields overnight, as if by magic. There have been nearly as many explanations put forward as there have been circles but no-one has yet 'proved' how these huge designs have been produced. It is true that there have been a few hoaxes, but these have been primitive and unimpressive compared with the many totally inexplicable examples. In recent years scientists have, perhaps somewhat reluctantly, taken part in some exploratory testing in order to shed light on their origins. No conclusive evidence has been provided and therefore what has been discovered has not been widely reported. The first acknowledgement is that no human activity has been detected. Scientific energy-measuring instruments, also dowsers, have found that the pattern can be mapped out by recording the increase in energy along the path of the pattern. This energy can still be detected after the field has been ploughed for at least two years following the formation of the pattern. The pattern is produced by heat, but the stems of the corn are not broken but folded and seed taken from the ears will produce a crop faster and larger than ordinary wheat grain, as though it had been irradiated.

There are no answers yet, but considerable speculation.

Today and Tomorrow

Governments undoubtedly keep the general population in ignorance. Over recent years there has been considerable evidence to suggest that scientific and technical development is far more advanced than the public is led to believe, but this knowledge is closely guarded by a powerful few. It is well known that Nikola Tesla's research into energy from the environment or 'free energy' was well advanced, as was his work on 'anti-gravity', and that all documentation on both topics was commandeered by the American Government and subsequently 'lost'.

One might question Governments' need for concern over these topics. It has even been suggested that Tesla had a uniquely brilliant mind and was possibly able to investigate knowledge that had been possessed by earlier Man and somehow lost, in much the same way as the skill of dowsing and faith healing has been lost for the majority of people.

As no-one, to date, has been able to adequately explain the building of the pyramids or the raising of the henges it may be just possible that people at the time had access to a knowledge of anti-gravity devices, which enabled them to complete what now seems an impossible task, and that knowledge was later lost.

Over the years the Churches have vigorously fought to subdue any information that might challenge their traditional teaching, but as previously mentioned, there were orders in the Church who knew and understood these matters. This has led to recent speculation that the Church's age-old quest for the 'Holy Grail' was not in fact a search for a precious golden chalice from which Christ had drunk. The Templars were clearly seeking something of great importance to them; something that would give them phenomenal power, perhaps the ancient knowledge of 'free energy'.

How the threads of earlier knowledge tie together we do not yet understand but we are learning continually more about the connections with our present understanding and the knowledge of the early mystics.

In this scientific age there is still a fear and denial of that which we do not fully understand. We have been tutored to expect proof and be wary and challenging in its absence. As scientific knowledge increases exponentially, from the amazing activity of inconceivably small particles at the interface of matter and energy in the Hadron project, to the unfolding of understanding of a Universe far vaster than can be comprehended, the more imaginative human mind wanders off into projections like, 'Star Wars', 'Avatar' and more.

At the time of writing, Hungarian researchers and others are delving into the mystery of 'dark energy' and the accelerated expansion of the Universe.

David Ergun investigates 'Umwelt' and the intensification of the interaction between our senses and their environment. Sensory substitution technology is progressing apace and with electronic chips in a simple bracelet it is possible to tap into parts of the brain normally unused, enabling the wearer to 'feel sounds', 'hear colours' and even to identify the eruption of a volcano over hundreds of miles.

Considerable work has been done in recent years in the field of subliminal conditioning techniques, which use parts of the brain not usually employed.

Oliver Sachs studied intensively the effects of damage to the frontal lobe of the human brain and found remarkable compensatory powers in numerous case studies, where patients showed extra-ordinary skills particularly in music and language, that they had not been aware of before. A completely unrelated part of the brain had been stimulated into action with startling consequences. Even this most brilliant and experienced neuro-scientist could not explain why this happens. We still understand very little about the interface between the brain and the mind: between the body and the spirit.

We can perhaps justifiably comment, 'there is more out there than meets the eye'.

Recently, the now late, Stephen Hawking was quoted as saying that in 10 years Man will have the ability to dematerialise. When Man has developed the ability to re-materialise, in the original form, then we will have entered the realms of 'Beam me up, Scotty', and will have the potential to move through space and time.

Interlude

"If you want to find the secrets of the
Universe, think in terms of energy,
frequency and vibration."

Nikola Tesla

"Enough!" some of you will be saying. You may already have found your long-held ideas challenged and believe our speculations to be the result of over-vivid imaginations.

You may wonder what all this has to do with dowsing for water, and the sceptics among you, quite rightly, will be looking for explanations that have a familiar ring – illusionism, unusual light effects, sleight of hand, autosuggestion, involuntary muscle twitch or just sheer chance. But to those who actually experience these phenomena, the effects are very real, and their cause is not easily dismissed.

Stay with us and share with us some of the many experiences we have had that have challenged our previous knowledge and baffled our comprehension.

Most of you will realise that so much of what has been mentioned so far can be linked by one word, ENERGY.

Whether it is the electromagnetic field produced by running water, the powerful earth energy lines, possibly related to the earth's magnetic field or nuclear activity in the sun, or even the energy generated by bodies and left residually in the ether by the spirit, our dowsers can identify it and, where necessary, interpret its meaning.

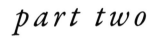

part two

Prelude

*It had snowed all day and in the late
afternoon the air over the lake was hazy. As
the light faded, a young girl appeared gliding
over the ice towards them but then, just as she
was within calling distance, she vanished.*

Those born with 'special' gifts, the ability to extend the sensitivity of their perception beyond the normal, to detect and identify energy and messages from nature that are beyond the expected, often exhibit no signs of these gifts in their early childhood. The development of their skills may be gradual and the magnitude of their powers vastly underestimated.

There are many who possess these skills but may, sadly, live an entire lifetime without knowledge of these gifts. The circumstances of their lives have provided no catalyst to spark the awakening of their inner depths. Their amazing light lies forever hidden under a bushel.

There are also those who show evidence of their unusual powers from early childhood. Although they may be aware that they are different, they may not understand why or how they are unlike those around them. These children may be absorbed by their own thoughts, sometimes oblivious of their surroundings. They are often highly imaginative. They may 'see' things invisible to others, and 'hear' sounds, perhaps voices, that others do not hear. They may truly 'see' fairies. These children may sometimes be described by parents, doctors and teachers as mildly autistic. But, while they are different and special, they are not sick or handicapped, they are privileged. They have extra-ordinary gifts which they can use to help others. They have the use of parts of their brains which, for most of us, are inaccessible. Many of these individuals will grow to be highly skilled detectors of earth energy in all its forms and also hypersensitive to the energy of spirits both alive and dead and will be drawn imperceptibly to all aspects of the paranormal.

The majority of people who would not consider that they have any 'special' powers will fall somewhere on a wide spectrum of sensitivity. It is our dowsers' experience that almost everyone, even the most ardent sceptic, is able to dowse at a basic level. Similarly, most people admit to being aware of positive or negative vibes when entering some properties. Our dowsers will show that these people are indeed picking up energy waves from earth energy or other sources.

So now we must start to identify what dowsing is, how it is done, and finally how it can be used.

Chapter One

- DOWSING? -
SKILL OR SCAM?

"Water, water, everywhere
Nor any drop to drink."
'The Rime of the Ancient Mariner'
Samuel Taylor Coleridge

The dictionary describes dowsing as the "search for underground water or minerals with the use of a divining rod".

But dowsing to a true dowser is far more than that. It is an intense sensitivity to the natural vibrations and rhythms of the earth and the spirit. While there is, still, in many quarters, scepticism and disbelief and the entire process has been debunked, it has also received considerable credibility. Serious documentary programmes have been made by the BBC and other respected networks around the world. Reputable newspapers like the Guardian and Times have carried articles covering the various activities of dowsers, and recently (2017) a new novel was published by Allan Mitchell, 'Sherlock Holmes and the Ley Line Murders'.

Most dowsers will use divining rods or other instruments like pendulums to access these energy sources, but there are others who feel these vibrations through their bodies with no mechanical aids. Most dowsers will have a favourite implement which works best for them. Some like to use bent metal rods, usually steel, aluminium, copper or brass, while others prefer forked twigs. These are flexible, wishbone-shaped, and often cut from local indigenous plants. In England willow and hazel are most commonly used, while our wizard uses alder in Canada and mimosa in Cyprus. According to Patrick Coyne in his article 'Mystery gift of dowsing' (Weekend Argus Feb 3rd 2018), dowsers in South Africa will use the unlikely materials cut from guava, mulberry or even oleander in spite of the poisonous properties of its sap. The force exerted on these forked twigs by a powerful energy field, whatever the source of the field, can be considerable. It can wrench the twig from the dowser's hand, snap the twig and even take the skin from the dowser's thumb. However, some dowsers use none of these, preferring to use metal pendulums, while others favour suspended crystals.

As underground flowing water produces a relatively strong electromagnetic field, detecting this is usually the starting point for the novice dowser. However, those who have true sensitivity soon progress to use their skills in a much wider sphere. Now that we have acknowledged that what is being detected is energy, then it is easier to understand how dowsers make the transfer from the purely practical, concrete substances into the realms of the spirit.

Research shows that dowsers have been, for many years, using their skills in numerous capacities that are not generally recognised.

In the oil industry throughout the world, while surveyors and technical soundings are used to locate oil and gas deposits, it is widely accepted that before drilling takes place a dowser is called in to finally confirm the exact spot for drilling. Drilling for oil is an expensive operation and mistakes cannot be made. (The use of dowsers in this industry was confirmed by a small boy, on an occasion when our dowser, 'Divine Bob', was demonstrating his skills to a group of school children. At question time a nine-year-old put up his hand to speak. He calmly dispelled all thoughts of wizardry when he confidently announced to all, that what Mr Bob had said was 'absolutely true', because he knew that his dad used dowsers at work in the oil fields in the Middle East.)

In the same way dowsers are called in to confirm the work of geologists in identifying seams of precious metals and gemstones in countries like South Africa and Russia.

During the last war dowsers were used by the War Office to locate the exact position of 'U' boats. Similarly, the American army used dowsers in the Vietnam War to track the underground tunnels used by the Vietcong to infiltrate American lines.

Finally, it is also known that the police, possibly as a last resort and certainly without any publicity, have used dowsers to track lost persons and also missing bodies. It is hard for a dowser, confident in his skills, to accept that his ability is viewed with deep scepticism by some authorities and the use of dowsers is rarely, if ever, admitted. Two infamous cases come to mind. The first is the Moors Murders. Both Hindley and Brady refused to disclose the location of the final body. It is, of course, possible that a dowser was used but, due to the lack of co-operation by the murderers, was sent to the wrong area. While the police apparently continued the search for years, there was never a report of a dowser being used.

Second was the high-profile case of Madeleine McCann. Considering the exceptionally high accuracy rate of many dowsers, it is remarkable that there was no report of a dowser being used to track her movements. If this was the case, it suggests culpable ignorance, gross incompetence or a monumental conspiracy and cover-up in high places.

<hr>

We have already inadvertently identified the main areas in which dowsers operate. They dowse for water, for minerals, archaeological sites, spiritual sites, bodies – alive and dead, and aspects of health, and our dowsers have experiences in all these areas, which they will share with you. But there is one highly advanced form of dowsing which our witch and wizard have mastered over time and that is called 'Remote Viewing', and more will be revealed of this technique later.

For would-be dowsers, it must always be remembered that they will be tapping into powerful forces that they are unlikely to understand. Whether they believe these energies are entirely a physical function of the earth's natural state or that they are in some way spiritual forces embedded in the earth by God or gods, there is a respect and a protocol. Even in the simplest and most mundane situation it is incumbent on the dowser to ask permission of Nature to explore and investigate. "May I, can I, should I?" is always asked before a dowse.

Even when this protocol has been vigorously observed, it may still be necessary, in some areas of high spiritual activity, where the energy forces are unknown, for dowsers to place themselves in a 'protective bubble'. There are a number of ways of achieving this, but the easiest and most popular is for the dowser to describe large circles in all three dimensions, to the extremes of their reach, thus forming an invisible sphere large enough to enclose them. Throughout the process they should be reciting an appropriate mantra, "Give me protection". They should then step inside their 'bubble' confident they will be protected from any malevolent forms of energy that may be present.

Initially a dowser using rods or forked twigs will have been taught how to hold his or her implements. The rods are held in a firm grip, but the thumbs must not cover the bend of the rod and so impede movement. The elbows should be tucked in tightly to the sides of the body and the rods held at right angles.

If twigs are being used the fork of the twigs should lie across upturned hands with the stem pointing out at right angles from the body. A mimosa twig, resting across two outstretched thumbs, will experience a downward force of nearly one Newton, when approaching a normal water course. This is strong enough to scrape skin from between the thumb and the index finger.

As the response to the stimuli can only be binary, the dowser's first task is to ascertain the rods' positive and negative response. Usually the rods will cross for 'Yes' and not react for 'No'. However, in some cases the rods may move outwards, and this is important to know. Similarly, if using twigs, they may move sharply downwards or upwards and, as this may be different for individuals, it is important to know what they are indicating.

Once the dowsing procedure starts it is vital that the questions put to the rods are clear and unambiguous and that the dowser is concentrating hard on the target. This precision will inevitably improve with experience. However, it is clear that the questioning is independent of language and the response will be the same regardless of the language used to the rods. This suggests that the skill being employed is one of consciousness and pre-dates language. It was used before Man had a spoken language, before the 'Tower of Babel'.

An advanced form of dowsing is remote dowsing or Remote Viewing. Some time ago, audiences were astonished watching a documentary on British television, in which a dowser was asked to pinpoint the position of a well several miles away. He was given an ordinance survey map of an area which was unfamiliar to him. He spread the map on the floor in his sitting room and taking out his rods he slowly scanned the map. Eventually his rods crossed, and he marked the exact spot beneath the rods. He scanned again and obtained the same result. He was then driven to the co-ordinates and the position of the well was confirmed without any doubt.

Remote Viewing involves picking up psychic signals from a distance and can be used to locate people or objects, and even for spying or espionage. It was given some credence, although without adequate explanation for most of the film-going public, in the Australian film 'The Water Diviner'. In the film, Joshua Connor (Russell Crowe), an Australian farmer and water dowser, loses his three sons at Gallipoli. Determined to find what happened to them, he 'Remote Views' and his mental images take him across the world, first to the site where two of them died on the Gallipoli peninsula, and then enabled him to find the third son.

This is not fantasy and the technique is widely used by the American Defence Intelligence Agency. Paul H Smith worked with the American Government's Remote Viewing programme in Ft Meade and has written extensively about his activities in volumes like 'Reading the Enemy's Mind: Inside Star Gate America's Psychic Espionage Programme' 2006. He has also produced a DVD on Dowsing and Remote Viewing Courses.

The ramifications are endless, and we will see as we follow our companions through their adventures, how, as their skills develop, they move into the realms of mental telepathy, regression, pranic healing and remote viewing.

When they first encounter these skills many people are nervous, some become excited. There are those who are extremely sceptical, when they find that there is no definitive scientific explanation of the phenomena. Some fear that practising such skills conflicts with their religious beliefs and yet others, many devout Christians, have no problem incorporating the idea of probing earth energy and even delving into the spirit world into their belief systems. It has been a constant source of surprise to our dowsers, the readiness they have witnessed, in members of eastern religions, to embrace the concepts of dowsing, and the easy and relaxed way these people accept the ideas.

Chapter Two

– A MODERN WIZARD –

Although our dowser, Bob, has ultimately developed his craft to a level where some of the skills he can demonstrate, and some of his experiences, could put him into a scene alongside Merlin and Gandalf, he did not graduate from Hogwarts and he had no knowledge of these gifts when he was young. He became a water diviner, or dowser, in a very practical situation.

It was in the early 1960s, de Havilland Aircraft industry, having been in the forefront of aviation development during the Second World War, with their German-defying 'Mosquito', were still investigating new methods of safely testing their aircraft frames to destruction. It was over 15 years since young Geoffrey de Havilland had been tragically killed when his plane, unable to absorb the stresses, disintegrated as he put it into a steep dive in an attempt to break the sound barrier. Only one year later the barrier was broken, and commercial, super-sonic flight became a possibility. At super-sonic speeds aircraft would have to withstand increasingly great stresses, strains and pressures, and so continuous testing was vital. The company had built a huge test tank capable of completely submerging a plane body in water. Testing could then take place under water, which would minimise the scattering of fragments at ultimate fatigue point and any explosive force would be contained. The tank was located on the company's Hatfield site. All that was needed to start testing was the water to fill the tank. Lea Valley Water Conservancy refused their permission for the company to draw from the municipal water supply the huge quantity of water necessary. The Authority did, however, grant them a permit to drill an Artesian well on the site, should a sufficient source of water be found there. Now the Company's problem was to find the water. A young structural engineer was detailed to find a dowser to discover any potential water supply. Duly, a dowser was employed and for two long days the young engineer followed the dowser as he meticulously surveyed the airfield.

Finally, a suitable source was found, but not before young Bob, fascinated by the skill and under the guiding hand of the experienced dowser, had tested his own ability and found that he too held the magic.

And so, our wizard now takes centre stage.

Bob was as surprised as anyone that he had the skill. He had known nothing of the dowsing art till that time.

As an only child in wartime, he was self-dependent, and self-sufficient. His family were not religious, and he was not reared in a spiritual environment. He was interested in and sensitive to nature but had not looked beyond the material world around him and would never have been considered contemplative. From childhood he had shown himself to be a doer rather than a dreamer and from an early age had the practical mind of an engineer. It was not the expected background of a would-be 'Wizard'.

At the time of his discovery, however, he was very engrossed in his career and although he was thrilled that he had 'the gift' he would not then have considered it a 'life defining' experience, and could not have imagined how this knowledge would one day completely change his life.

In fact, the event was almost forgotten, and it was some years later when he was collecting a couple of sail boards from a warehouse in the Midlands that the company director shared a banal problem with him. The Health and Safety Inspector had told him that he would have to put in another toilet for his staff, to comply with regulations. A problem arose when the only area of his premises that could be allocated for the facility had no obvious water supply. The warehouse owner knew that there was a capped-off water pipe under the main floor, but the very old building plan did not show its location. He faced the cost of having to dig up the entire concrete floor in order to find the pipe. He was not happy! Fortunately, he had spoken to the right person, and Bob, remembering his earlier experience, was confident that the rods would indicate the position of the pipe. Acquiring a couple of lengths of welding rods, they bent them into right angles in the vice and Bob went to work. He walked slowly up and down across the floor, concentrating hard on asking the rods to show him the position of the water pipes. He made a chalk mark every time the rods crossed. Having covered the entire area, he joined the marks and was convinced that the line showed the path of the water pipe. When the contractors chipped away the concrete at the end of the line only the owner was astonished that they had revealed the end of the pipe. Delighted that he had been saved a considerable sum of money, he asked Bob what he charged. The thought of remuneration had never crossed our wizard's mind and he went home very happy in the possession of two large cans of wood preserver for his services.

The years rolled by and he dowsed for water occasionally if friends, both in England and in Canada, needed to dig a well. There was nothing very exciting even though other people found the skill remarkable and, through their awe, he became more conscious of his own exceptional ability. Certainly, he knew that he was becoming more sensitive to the vibrations he was feeling when dowsing, and he began to question where this energy was coming from, what was its source. He had realised that the more he worked his skill the more sensitive he became. He could now not only find water courses, cables and pipes, but he could give their depth to an amazing accuracy. He astonished himself when he first found that the precision of the questions he asked the rods defined the accuracy of their response. He found that he could walk over an underground stream that his rods had just identified, with no response from the rods, if he was asking them to identify an electric cable. He then discovered a method of calculating the depth of an underground stream and from that, the depth the digger or driller would have to go to find the water for a well.

He would mark the direction of flow of the stream, and then walk away at right angles to the flow asking the rods to indicate the depth. He marked the position where the rods crossed and then measured the distance between the mark and the position of the flow. This distance was unfailingly found to be the depth of the water.

As his sensitivity increased, he discovered that just by standing over the flow, merely asking the rods for the depth and counting, in either feet or metres, the rods would cross decisively at the appropriate number.

Over the years, professional well-diggers have been amazed at the uncanny accuracy of his 'prediction' and while, at first, they were dismissive – particularly if they were required to drill through hard rock, to reach the required depth, they soon came to respect his insistence that they continue drilling!

The use of this ability alone has helped so many people and solved a few irritating problems.

Our wizard's family, although they had heard of his early experience, had little understanding of the extent of his powers, and like him had almost forgotten about it over time.

One weekend they were invited to stay with old friends at their beautiful Sussex home. The property was large with several acres of land and two small lakes. It was a glorious June Saturday afternoon and they all sat in the gazebo on the lawn with their tea and cakes. Peter chatted with Bob about his management of the land and then, with no knowledge of Bob's skills, shared with him a problem that had been troubling him. His larger lake was being polluted with a strange scum and he had no idea of its source. Bob boldly announced to an astonished Peter and doubtful listeners, that he could discover the cause of the problem. Celia was duly dispatched to the house for a spare pair of Aero, aluminium knitting needles, which were bent to the appropriate angle. Our dowser needed nothing else, he was ready to perform. It made an amusing scene as he strode confidently across the lawn, like the Pied Piper, gathering behind him the three incredulous adults, three inquisitive teenagers, Lindy, a large and ponderous cream Labrador, a sprightly and nosey, curly dachshund, trotting purposefully behind her adored mistress, and finally the family's ginger Tom, whose curiosity overcame his aged dignity. And so, they proceeded, surprisingly, not towards the lake but straight for Celia's kitchen garden. (Bob admitted afterwards that he realised he was asking the rods the wrong question.) While the others looked decidedly sceptical, Peter had turned a 'lighter shade of pale'. Only he knew that, years earlier, when they had first purchased the property, he had filled in an ancient, defunct well, in the centre of where the kitchen garden then stood and at the precise position that the rods were indicating. The rods did not err, they had not been asked the right question and had led to the original position of the well, under which the old stream still flowed.

Realising his mistake, Bob amended his questioning and was soon able to give his friend the bad news that the pollution was caused by a flow of effluent draining under the adjacent road from a farm on the other side. It is perhaps an understatement to record that the onlookers were impressed.

Chapter Three

– A LATTER-DAY WITCH –

During the period of Bob's life when he was working tirelessly to develop a new career and support his young family, with little time even to remember, let alone practise, his dowsing skills, some hundred miles to his north, a little girl, much the same age as his own children, played innocently among the rolling hills of Worcestershire. It was an ideal life for a natural country child, who loved the freedom of the great outdoors. The diminutive figure, with a blazing halo of golden hair glinting red in the sun, and piercing green eyes, that saw far beyond the normal horizon, was often spotted by the locals, roaming the fields and hillsides. But this was no ordinary child. From a very early age she showed signs of being 'different'. Elderly aunts and neighbours would shake their heads sagely and mutter, "That child's been here before". She was very advanced and spoke well before the average child. As a two-year-old, she worried her grandmother with her old woman mannerisms, wringing her hands and shaking her head, as though she was deep in stressful thoughts, way beyond the present.

While she appeared a solitary soul to distant observers she was not 'alone'. Many children have imaginary pets or 'friends', but for Susy they were truly 'real'. She can never remember being without her constant companion, Julian. She could clearly see Julian beside her, even before she could speak. As she grew older, she was so convincing, that her vision of Julian became accepted by the family, and, on her insistence, a place would always be laid at the table for him. Similarly, she would refuse to board a bus until her mother had also paid for a ticket for Julian.

She had a little cat at home but there was no dog in the house, that is, apart from Gego, a little grey, wire-haired terrier. Neither her parents, nor her younger sister ever saw Gego, and yet he was ever-present. Susy would talk to him incessantly and can describe him in vivid detail to this day.

In the early days, Susy's mother indulged what she saw as her bright little daughter's fantasies. However, she began to realise that the child's 'unusual' behaviour could cause a problem if it continued when Susy started school. She set out then with a firm determination to stop 'all this nonsense'. She suddenly metamorphosed into a strict disciplinarian, getting cross if Julian or Gego were mentioned. She would shout at the small, bewildered child to, "Stop lying – you don't want people to think you are a liar". Meanwhile, however, Susy's sensitivity and perception had moved on to another level and her innocent observation, "That woman's all green!" would inevitably provoke a smack. Too young to understand her mother's concerns, she became wary of people's reactions and so grew to be shy and introverted.

At school, her shyness was misinterpreted as standoffishness and she was generally shunned by the other children. She made no friends throughout her school years and worse, she was bullied by both pupils and teachers. Soon after she transferred to secondary school, she discovered she had attracted the unwelcome attention of a group of older bullies, who would waylay her in the corridors and stick pins in her. Even one of her teachers would 'pick on her' and unnervingly stare at her in class. It is little wonder that, despite being clever and a top-stream pupil, she hated school and could not wait to leave.

Looking back, she realises that she was giving off unseen vibes that unnerved and unsettled others. They feared the hidden depths that they did not comprehend, and their apprehension caused them to take aggressive action.

She was conscious, as a teenager, that she was highly electrostatically charged and would regularly give anyone close to her a sudden, sharp shock.

Even when she started work she was conscious that her colleagues treated her differently. They seemed to challenge an unseen part of her character that they did not understand. She felt they pushed and tested her to see how far they could go before she snapped and revealed the part of herself that she was keeping from them.

As her self-possession grew, so her psychic skills developed. She recalls that even at college, she had the power to exercise control over others. When sitting on a bus, she could call up enough psychic energy to send the passenger sitting next to her to sleep. She now understands that this is done by synchronising breathing patterns and believes it would be an invaluable tool for dentists who operate on anxious patients.

At times of great stress or anger, she has consciously cleared a complete aisle in a busy supermarket, simply by using the mental power of her emotional venom to summon up sufficient psychic force.

Eventually, scared by the enormity of her growing psychic potential, and realising the power she had at her disposal to exert for good or evil, she made a conscious decision to deny the force and so, while still little more than a girl, she locked it away in a casket to be re-opened later like Pandora's Box.

Chapter Four

– A RETURN TO BASIC DOWSING –

It was not until he retired from work and put behind him the stresses and time commitment of the work-a-day world that Bob was able to renew his interest in dowsing and further develop his talent to a level he would have thought impossible.

The Mediterranean island of Cyprus provided him with numerous opportunities to hone his skills. Had he been looking for fame and notoriety he would have had a lucky break. He had dowsed wells for a few friends, when a well-known local radio presenter overheard him relating his experiences, at a party. The presenter was fascinated by what she was hearing. Always on the look-out for new material and guests for her broadcast, she introduced herself and invited Bob to appear on the programme. It was Northern Cyprus's version of 'Desert Island Discs'. The guests were interviewed about their lives and interests and the discourse was punctuated by the guests' pre-chosen favourite music. Although confident in his knowledge and enthusiasm, Bob had little experience of public speaking and none of live broadcasting. He was highly impressed by the professionalism of the presenter and the level of research she had obviously done in order to, so competently, plan her questions.

The programme was widely supported by ex-pats and it was soon clear that everyone he knew, and many more, had listened to the programme. He was soon receiving phone calls from complete strangers, including several building contractors.

During the housing boom of the early 2000s he was in constant demand by new house-buyers to locate water for their wells. Home-owners were not allowed to use their municipal water supply to water their gardens and fill their swimming pools, so a well was an economically preferable option to bringing in the tanker.

While dowsing for well water can be a routine and somewhat unimaginative occupation, Bob's experiences were often enlivened by meeting so many interesting members of the delightfully eclectic population of Turkish Cyprus. Some provided amusing incidents while others related tales from their past. His activities were often observed by some mystified but many enthusiastic locals and gardeners, who could not believe that he was only seeking water. Most were entirely convinced that he was in search of oil or gold.

However, his experiences were nearly halted permanently by an unsettling event soon after he arrived at his new home. He was invited by an acquaintance, who had been a resident ex-pat for some years, to dowse his land in an attempt to discover why a previously active well appeared dry. Surveying the area, he suspected that the supply stream had diverted. This often occurred due to even slight earth tremors or more frequently to extensive rock mining in the vicinity. Eventually he picked up a stream, and followed by his usually coterie of fascinated observers he tracked it downhill. Suddenly, without the usual vibrational warning, the rods went berserk. Bob simultaneously experienced a sharp and frightening sensation in his left arm (he is left-handed). He tried to drop the rod but found he could not loosen his grip. It was like rigor mortis. The shocked observers reported later that his face drained of every vestige of colour and he appeared on the point of losing consciousness. It was feared he was having a stroke. Fortunately, the spasm was transient, his colour returned, and he was able to resume his investigation. At that point the old gardener appeared and removed some stones and boarding, unknown to the house-owner, and revealed an even older well that was believed defunct, but over time had collected seepage and was holding about 25m depth of water.

It proved an interesting discovery, but also a salutary lesson that the dowser is working with powerful forces that can, under certain circumstances, adversely affect his own physiology, and precautions must be taken. From that point Bob has always ensured that his body is fully hydrated before he dowses and invariably rests afterwards.

Bob was soon astonished to find that most of his clients, mainly retired, if not ancient, Brits appeared to believe that the island was floating on a lake of fresh water. He was called to one home, an attractive modern house on a small estate, with the usual donum (third of an acre) of land immaculately landscaped. The front of the house was neatly paved with an elaborate and obviously expensively built 'feature' in front of the main entrance. In the corner was a delightful, traditionally decorated 'wishing well', which to the owner's horror had proved to yield no water. Bob, rods in hand, strode the site. There was no underground stream in the vicinity of the well. He asked who had suggested that the £5000 worth of well be placed in its present position. The wife, blushingly, admitted that she had wanted it there as it looked pretty! Bob continued his survey of the property and all was not lost as there was a quite strong stream flowing through, but it came down the mountain, straight under the house, and, I'm sure many of you will be ahead of me here, straight under the middle of the exotic garden feature. A very costly error indeed!

On other occasions Mother Nature herself has played a devious role. He was called one day to, again, a new home. This time the owners had taken the precaution of seeking the advice of the builder's surveyor. In truth, these professionals, even if they are not themselves dowsers, have a good working knowledge of water courses and the direction of their flow. The well, in question, was strategically placed in the far corner of the garden, to be jointly used, and paid for, by friends in the adjoining property. It had been sited exactly as suggested by the surveyor and it had yielded no water. Our dowser paced the land and marked the flow. A projection showed that the well was appropriately placed. He then checked the depth of the underground stream and the owners confirmed that the well had been dug to that depth. For once our dowser was mystified. His assessment had never failed before, but this time he initially admitted to being baffled. Then, he had a thought! Because it was so near to the corner of the land he had not taken the trouble to follow the stream to the exact spot of the well but had tracked the line of the stream down the mountain and projected it. He retraced his steps to his last point marked and continued his checks every metre until he was within a couple of metres of the well. Then suddenly the water disappeared! Of course, it had not vanished but so very near to the well, the stream had hit a layer of hard rock and had naturally diverted at right angles, swinging away from the hole and depriving the well of its feed. Nature laughed, but at least the mystery was solved. All was not lost as the water was not far from the hole, and the neighbours had the opportunity to share a little more expense and dig sideways into the flow and so secure their plentiful supply.

On this occasion both the clients were keen to test their skills with the rods and both were successful. The wife then admitted that, while she had not used rods before, she had for many years used a pendulum and fervently believed that through this instrument she had made spiritual contact with a recently departed aunt.

One day Bob was asked to dowse a large piece of land, about eight acres, on behalf of a property developer. The land was on a hillside with spectacular views of both mountains and sea. The owner planned to split the land into five, potentially very valuable, lots. However, he needed to be sure that there was water available. He had already paid out a considerable sum to a local technical surveyor, who, using electrical resistance techniques to determine the presence of water, had told him there was none. Not satisfied with this assessment, the developer had called in the true expert! In a relatively short time Bob had confirmed that there was an adequate supply of water on four of the five plots. The delighted developer then went ahead and built his exclusive homes confident that they would never suffer a water shortage and to this day, some ten years later, they certainly have not.

As his reputation grew he found he was travelling further afield and the scope of his dowsing was increasing.

He was surprised, one day, to receive a phone call from an unknown gentleman, who explained that he had been given Bob's number by a lady he was talking to while standing in the queue at a bank in a city, 10 miles away. (She had not given her name and her identity has never been discovered.) The elderly gentleman was a retired judge and came from the village in Karpaz known as 'Judges' Village', so called because many of the sons of the village over the years had become judges. The judge had large tracts of land around the village and needed water. They arranged to meet in Famagusta the following day and the judge drove Bob to his land. It did not take our wizard long to find the first stream and that was to be one of many he located that day to the delight of the judge. Interested in the direction of one of the underground streams, Bob decided to follow it and, stalked closely by the fascinated client, he made his way across a field. Having laboriously crossed several fields and panted over rocky outcrops, they eventually found themselves on the beach, where to Bob's delight and his companion's amazement, they found the stream bubbling to the surface through the sand, in a spring of fresh water. The judge admitted that even though he had played on the beach throughout his childhood and visited the area regularly, he had never spotted the spring.

The judge was so excited by their discovery and the very satisfactory results, that he insisted on treating the dowser to a meal in the village restaurant, where he met all the old locals and was regaled with tales of the 'good old days' in the village. Bob arrived home exhausted, but he had certainly had a memorable day and one he often likes to recall.

Not all stories were happy ones and sometimes he had to give clients bad news. He was called to one home where the couple were hoping to open an animal rescue centre but needed to have their own water supply as their requirements would be great and tanker water would be prohibitively expensive.

They were a friendly young couple who had only recently arrived on the island, seeking the sun. They were happy to chat away about their former employment. They had been resident house-keeper and general factotum at a baronial mansion in Scotland, belonging to a very well-known and much-loved celebrity. They spoke highly and most colourfully of their charismatic employers who, actually, spent most of their time in America and used the Scottish mansion mainly for entertaining guests. This meant that their house-keepers (we'll call them Kate and Steve) spent a considerable amount of time on the large property on their own. They enjoyed walking the extensive woods and soon made the acquaintance of the kitchen staff at an adjoining, even larger estate. Kate found that she was readily welcomed as a regular visitor for morning coffee. Wandering in the woods in the early morning she came upon a spot where there were numerous chanterelles. She collected these and arrived at the neighbour's kitchen with a full basket. The cook was delighted, and willingly paid her the market price saying that, as the master loved them, she would buy as many as Kate could supply. Sometime later Kate was, again, sitting in the kitchen, enjoying her coffee, the large basket of mushrooms on the table, when the door opened and in walked Prince Charles. (She was, in fact, in the kitchen at Balmoral.) The Prince spied the basket and beamed at her, warmly thanked her for her efforts and insisted she visited whenever she liked, preferably with a basket of his favourite food. While honoured to have been noticed by the Prince, she was highly embarrassed at the time, although she could laugh about it later, as the mushrooms, unknown to the Prince or his trusting Cook, were in fact picked from a glade on a remote fringe of the Balmoral Estate itself.

While Bob had thoroughly enjoyed his visit and meeting this lively and enthusiastic young couple, sadly he had to tell them that there was not enough water on their property for their needs and eventually they gave up their plans and moved to Turkey.

Other dowsing experiences came from unexpected quarters. Shortly after moving to Cyprus he decided to take a skiing holiday in Turkey. At the hotel, he was befriended by the young Head Waiter, Huseyin. It transpired that Huseyin, despite working annually at a ski resort, had never skied. Bob endeared himself to the young man by taking him and another young waiter to the slopes on their free afternoon and teaching them the rudiments of skiing. Both young men loved the experience and became enthusiastic down-hillers. Some months later Bob received an urgent invitation to visit Huseyin's family in Mersin. The three siblings and their partners were all gathering at their parents' house and Huseyin was anxious that they should all meet his new English friend. Bob travelled across on the hydrofoil to Tascacu where he was met by the father, Halil, a former policeman. The family were delightful and made Bob extremely welcome. Halil's wife Mediha worked miracles of culinary magic in her tiny and sardine-packed apartment. On the first evening, the conversation moved to dowsing and, to the amazement of his sons, Halil admitted that he, too, was a dowser. None of the family had any idea that he had this skill. It transpired that he and Bob dowsed in an identical way and had identical reactions. The evening was then spent in a variety of dowsing 'party games'. To his own astonishment, Bob found that he could find different items that had been hidden, including a lump of sugar. He had, up to then, believed that items being dowsed had to produce an obvious electromagnetic field, like running water or electricity, or at least had to be in some way an electrical conductor. He then realised that with sufficient sensitivity it was possible to pick up the minute field produced around any object or material due to the natural movement of the electrons within the atoms of the substance.

The visit had been a delightful social experience, but Bob left a more insightful dowser than when he arrived, and marvelled that fate had brought him into contact with a similar, yet more skilful diviner.

While the demand for water kept him busy, he was also refining his skills and he then realised that his special sensitivity would take him into realms not yet investigated.

As Bob became well known throughout the TRNC as a reliable water diviner, interest in his skill grew and he was invited to give an illustrated talk to the local Anglo-Turkish Association. Though initially a little nervous, he was keen to share his experiences with others. However, when the talk was publicised in the local newspaper, there was an outcry from the Authorities and they tried to get the presentation cancelled. The reason given was that there was a shortage of water and once everyone knew how to dowse they would be digging their own wells. Bob did not believe a word of it. Firstly, there were strict rules already in place controlling the granting of a licence for a well and secondly, his many dowsing experiences had convinced him that there was no shortage of water on his side of the island and that most people could benefit from sinking a well into the surface water that would otherwise flow to the sea.

(In TRNC, domestic wells can be sunk to a depth not exceeding 35m. Depths below this would encroach on the official aquifers from which the authorities draw the town water. As this is being written the situation is changing due to the new water supply from Turkey.)

The real reason for the complaint was never disclosed but one can only speculate that some in high places had a vested interest in the electrical resistance technique for locating water.

In the event, the pressure group's objections were over-ridden and the talk went ahead. They say that all publicity is 'good' publicity and this certainly appeared so in this case. Following a double page spread in the English language newspaper, it turned out to be one of the best attended presentations enjoyed by the Association. Bob talked in general about his background in dowsing, introduced his audience to the various methods and tools of dowsing and then demonstrated searches for water and electricity cables. A high spot in the evening occurred when Bob was using a forked mimosa branch to show the effect, when he approached an electric power cable. He steadily walked towards the power cable which supplied the microphone speaker and gradually the branch moved between his hands. The hushed crowd watched mesmerised as the branch quivered, bending strongly and forcing downwards against the supporting pressure. Then, inadvertently, Bob took a step nearer the speaker and the silence was broken by a sharp electric crackle, the rod snapped and flew from his hands and nearly a hundred people gasped in shock. After that his entire audience was rapt and everyone wanted to be a dowser. All had been invited to bring along their own BBQ skewers, bent to an 'L' shape, in case they wished to 'have a go', and when the talk finally ended, and the many questions had been answered, it was amusing to watch so many 'would-be' dowsers pacing the hallways and patios of the venue concentrating hard on their skewers and pleading for water.

With an average annual rainfall in the TRNC of a mere 402mm, it is hard to imagine the source of the water flowing constantly from the Kyrenia range to the sea. The vast increase in population over the last 20 years could have put unsupportable demands on the water supply, and yet most wells continue to flow even in the driest seasons.

In one case the water had been located on a property close to the house. Bob was most specific about the depth and insisted that the client supervise the drilling and make sure that the appropriate level was reached. (This is always important as some drillers will take the first sign of damp grey clay as the indicator of water and will stop drilling even though the dowser may have given a greater depth for the main flow. Also, the drillers are reluctant to go through bedrock as it wears out their expensive drill bits, but the main flow may be below the rock.) In this instance the client allowed the driller to stop prematurely and even set in the supporting rings. Having already paid over a considerable amount of money, he was extremely disappointed with the volume of his supply. When Bob was approached he was quite vexed, as it was immediately obvious that the correct depth had not been reached. After much soul searching, the client reluctantly agreed to the expensive task of having the rings removed and bringing the drill back to finish the job. The task was finally finished to our dowser's satisfaction and within a month the, then delighted, client was able to report an amazing flow of water that had enabled him, despite the large usage by his B and B business, to be independent of the municipal supply.

This was one of many similar cases, and so with such a modest rainfall and what appeared a disproportionate supply on the island, it led Bob to question the source.

For a long time he had believed that much of the water came from natural springs, high up in the Kyrenia Mountains, and yet he could not believe that these springs were kept running by the intermittent rainfall. He became totally convinced that these springs were fed by powerful streams of fresh water flowing deep under the Mediterranean from the Taurus Mountains in southern Turkey and forced into the Kyrenia range by hydrostatic pressure. This theory has been propounded by others but has also been denied by some schools of geology.

However, Bob considers he has two quite strong pieces of evidence to support this theory. The first was supplied by a novice dowser, when he inadvertently discovered something that Bob had missed. It was not unusual for Bob to fall upon unsuspecting visitors, thrust a pair of barbecue skewers into their hands, tuck their elbows neatly into their ribs and send them off across his field chanting the mantra "show me water, show me water!"

This sunny Saturday afternoon, however, he had one eager acolyte. Heidi was excited and could not wait to test her skills. She soon found she was a natural, picking up both water courses and electric cables with ease. Her husband, Dick, on the other hand, was very different. He shrank into the background and refused to touch the proffered rods. Despite constant exhortation from his exhilarated wife, his reluctance persisted. Ultimately curiosity overcame his nervousness and he submitted to instruction. He then approached the task with the intensity of a perfectionist bordering on the paranoid. His concentration almost reached a point of 'lock-out'. In spite of this, or even perhaps because of it, he crossed two surface-water streams without a reaction from the rods. He continued walking and just when Bob was about to intervene, the rods crossed vigorously. Bob was seen shaking his head doubtfully, as he had never been aware of a watercourse at that point on his land, but he paid Dick the respect of checking his findings. To his amazement his rods confirmed the presence of a powerful flow of water. Believing that he had checked his property thoroughly for all so-called surface water he then experienced a frisson of excitement. As everyone watched, he asked the rods to indicate the direction of the flow and to their astonishment the rod showed the water travelling away from the sea towards the mountain. Suspecting then what had been discovered, he checked the depth to find that the flow was an incredible 50m below the surface. The novice dowser had almost certainly, unwittingly, proved the presence of the legendary water course under the sea, feeding a spring in the mountains behind the house. Where there is one such stream there could be many more waiting to be discovered.

Supplementary, if circumstantial, evidence came from observation of his own well. The well had provided water consistently over ten years or so, but, one exceptionally dry summer the flow slowed down. By the end of September, the decrease in volume was cause for concern, with still no rain in the forecast. Then suddenly, and at first unaccountably, the volume improved dramatically even though the island had experienced no rainfall and even the night dews had not started. It was a mystery, and yet for Bob, it was a mystery quickly solved when he remembered that a couple of weeks earlier there had been torrential rain in the Taurus Mountains in southern Turkey. He was then convinced that his theory was vindicated.

Like most enthusiasts, Bob would never miss an opportunity to share his knowledge and skills with others, and so he was pleased to be invited by a local school to take part in the children's project on water. It had been many years since he had stepped into a classroom and he approached with caution and a liberal dose of apprehension, when he found himself confronted by fifty pairs of interested but challenging eyes.

The children had been well prepared by their previous experiences and had a good working knowledge of the importance of water in our lives and also the mechanics of the water cycle. Bob explained about dowsing and then took them out on to the school field to demonstrate finding an underground stream. He used the children as markers to denote the direction and the width of the water course and showed them how he determined the depth. The children loved being involved and a few of them tested their own skill with the rods and a couple of them proved to be natural dowsers. The practical activity was followed by a plenary session and the youngsters enthusiastically vied for his attention as they asked their amazingly perceptive questions. Bob was delighted by the eager participation and understanding of these intelligent young people. He was confident that he had given them a key, which perhaps in years to come would open a door to many of the wonders that he, himself, had experienced.

Chapter Five

– ONE THING LEADS –
TO ANOTHER

It was a cool day in late spring and Bob was busy at his annual task, lumber-jacking, in his Canadian woodland. It was almost lunch-time when his chainsaw finally ran out of fuel. Planning to complete his task after he had eaten, he carried his chainsaw back to his garage to re-fill its tank. To his intense annoyance he noticed a nut was missing from the outer casing. Having no idea when the nut had fallen off, he felt he had no chance of finding it. This caused considerable frustration as it was over an hour's drive to the nearest 'local' chainsaw supplier. He sulked throughout his lunch and then had an inspiration. For some unexplained reason he remembered his trip to Mersin the previous winter and recalled finding the sugar lump with the rods. If he could find a sugar lump then, just maybe, he could find the chainsaw nut. With renewed enthusiasm, he returned to the tree he had been felling. Only then was he aware of the enormity of the task and the improbability of success. He had been working over a large area of natural woodland and he had no idea at which point the nut had dropped. The forest floor was carpeted with twigs and leaves several inches deep. Despair returned and yet he realised that there was nothing to be lost. He took up his rods, with little hope, and began carefully walking the area. His perseverance was rewarded when, to his amazement, the rods homed in on a particular spot. However, no nut was visible. He approached again from a different angle, and again the rods indicated the same spot. Feeling confidence in his rods returning, he knelt at the spot and gently lifted the leaves from the surrounding surface, and there, to his utter astonishment, was the nut.

The relating of this tale brought him numerous requests to find lost items, but these were mostly unrealistic and so not all his searches were successful.

On two separate occasions he was asked to dowse for diamonds that had been lost from rings, but they had been mislaid many months earlier and in neither case was it known exactly when or where the gems had been lost. Sadly, all the rods could do was to confirm that neither of the stones was in the vicinity of the owners' homes.

Possibly the most bizarre request was to find a pair of mislaid false teeth. Fortunately, before he could set out, he received a call to say they had been located.

While he never discovered anything of great value, the rods performed wonders in helping him locate tools that had been carelessly dropped down and frustratingly forgotten.

This formed the basis of a new entertainment, the dowser's version of 'hide and seek'.

He soon realised that, if, as he had demonstrated, the rods could identify and locate a vast variety of items, then maybe they could also identify and locate people.

He started tentatively by asking the rods to point to named people in the room, which they did unerringly. Conscious that he may be influencing the rods, he repeated the test blind-folded and asked people to change their positions. Again, the rods were faultless and 'Voila!' the dowsers' 'Blind Man's Bluff' was born.

The next stage was to test this ability over a distance, by asking the rods to indicate if certain named people were at their homes. Conscious of the scepticism of many and the accusation that the results were mere chance, he tested it numerous times with many different people and followed up with a phone call to check and both in Cyprus and Canada he was never wrong.

He was demonstrating this one evening after dinner and a guest asked if he could tell him the location of a named acquaintance unknown to Bob. Bob was hesitant but thought he could do it by concentrating on the guest as a 'go-between'. The rods, without hesitation, pointed down the coast to the east and Bob suggested that the subject was in Esentepe, a village some 12km to the east. "Yes," said the guest pleased with the confirmation, as he had already suspected the fellow's whereabouts, "I know that! But can you give me a precise address?"

Bob knew that this level of detail, from that distance, was beyond his skill at that time. However, the guest sighed and then laughed, declaring that it was a pity, as the fellow owed him quite a lot of money!

But not everyone is convinced. Even when they see the evidence, they cannot accept there is no trickery.

As a dinner party guest himself, one evening Bob was pressed to demonstrate his skills. He did a few water and cable locations then said he would check to see if the neighbours were at home. He had driven past the home in question on his way to dinner and as there were no cars in the drive and no signs of life, he thought he already knew the answer to his question. In fact, several of the dinner guests believed the family to be away on holiday. Bob went ahead and asked the rods, which immediately indicated that the family were at home. Mumbles of disagreement spread around the room and the host quite red with indignation declared the whole idea a farce. After all, everyone knew the neighbours were away! Bob, who always believed his rods, continued in the face of universal disbelief, to maintain that they were at home. Meanwhile, another guest was on the phone to the family and was heard assuring them that he wasn't planning to call in, but merely checking that they were indeed at home. It turned out that everyone was mistaken and only the rods were correct, as the neighbours had only been out to the shops, and were not going on holiday until the following week. Everyone was most impressed except the host, who maintained his opinion and, to this day, views the whole idea of dowsing with considerable misgiving.

While these apparent party games undoubtedly entertain, they are never used to trivialise or undervalue the power of the energy forces at work. The dowser seeks only to demonstrate the range and scope of these forces at a basic level and by doing so he introduces the concept of dowsing to many people who would not normally have any knowledge or understanding of these skills, and some go on to discover their own, formerly hidden, abilities.

Chapter Six

– ASSOCIATED PHENOMENA –

As his first-hand dowsing experiences challenged him to research the source of the energy he was detecting, Bob found he was being directed to a vast array of other forms of unexplained energy that he would not have assumed were related. He became increasingly interested in other strange phenomena, particularly UFO sightings, corn circles and ghosts.

While he did believe that he had seen a UFO, he had never seen a ghost. However, he came to realise that, over many years, others had seemed drawn to share their paranormal experiences with him.

Even as a school boy he was made party to a weird experience of his two best friends. The three boys would often play in the woods on the edges of the park around Hatfield House in Hertfordshire, the ancestral home of Lord Salisbury and the Cecil family. It was at the far end of the park where it sweeps down to the river and the Broadwater Lake that Bob was first made aware of the 'other world'.

Although this was merely a second-hand encounter it had a remarkable effect on him and in later years he told the story often as he became increasingly conscious of his own hypersensitivity to the paranormal.

It was a snowy winter day and as the lake was frozen the two brothers, Richard and Vernon, were planning to skate on the frozen water. It was late in the afternoon and the light was hazy. As Vernon stooped to fix his skates, Richard appeared distracted even mesmerised by something he saw at the end of the lake. He described the scene to his brother. He had seen a girl, dressed like a servant, perhaps a hundred years earlier, slowly moving through the mist. As the light faded, she glided over the ice towards them but then, just as she was within calling distance she vanished. Completely convinced that Richard had seen a ghost, the boys could not wait to get to school the next day to tell their friends, including Bob, of their experiences. The news spread around the school like a forest fire and it was not long before it reached the ears of the Headmaster who called the brothers to his study and severely reprimanded them for telling stories that caused consternation to some of the other pupils. The boys strongly avowed the truth of their tale. As the lads were usually trustworthy, the wise Headmaster decided to investigate for himself. Taking note of all the details from the boys he repaired to the library where he did some local research, and his findings were astounding.

He discovered that in the previous century the river had been diverted to provide a mill stream and at the position where Richard declared he had first seen the girl there had been a bridge. Closer investigation into the social history of the area revealed that in the mid-nineteenth century a serving girl at the House had been seduced by a male member of the family and found herself in the family way. Unable to bear the shame she had thrown herself from the bridge and drowned at the very spot where Richard had seen her. There was then little doubt in the Head's mind that the boys had indeed seen the spirit of the girl and he called them in and apologised for not believing them in the first instance.

◄━━━►

Many years later Bob was supporting a pair of paddlers in the Devizes to Westminster kayak race. This gruelling marathon covering 125 miles, first on the Kennet-Avon canal and then joining the Thames at Reading, has taken place every Easter weekend since 1948. The kayakers have to carefully choose their departure time and calculate their expected speed of paddling, in order to maximise the effect of the tide when reaching the final tidal stretch of the Thames. They paddle through the night and every boat will have a support team that will drive the distance, stopping at intervals to intercept their paddlers to supply food, drink and sometimes dry clothing. Dead of night on the river can be an eerie experience and support teams guard against using strong torches and flash-lights as they can be disorienting. On this occasion Bob and the other two members of the team had placed themselves on Staines Bridge. The darkness and silence were palpable. Bob strained his eyes into the pitch black up-river in the hope of seeing his paddler. Turning away from the water to rest his eyes, he was stunned to see a brilliant light high up in the sky. He drew the attention of his companions to the strange phenomenon, which was so high it appeared to be beyond the atmosphere. It was moving towards the earth at an incredible rate. Thinking it must be a meteorite, they were astounded when, as it suddenly swung over on to its side, catching the sun, it appeared oval and enormous in size. Still moving at an unbelievable speed, it turned at right angles to its original path and disappeared from view. It was no meteorite and to this day Bob is totally convinced that what they saw that night was a 'flying saucer', an extra-terrestrial craft.

It was a very ordinary, rather cold, damp morning at the very end of November. Bob was in his office putting together an order, when Sharon, from the company next door, ran in to tell him that she and her husband, Alan, had had a weird and quite scary experience on the previous evening. They were about to tell the story to their colleagues and invited him in to their office to listen. They had been driving home to Boreham Wood after a night out with friends in London. They were just driving past Arkley golf course when they both noticed a fierce fire burning at the far end of a field. At first, they drove on, but very shortly Sharon felt concerned and wondered if there was anyone there that needed help, so Alan turned the car and returned to the spot where they had seen the blaze. To their utter disbelief, there was no sign of any fire. Their genuine bewilderment was obvious as they told the tale.

Throughout the telling, their office manager had sat at his desk silent. When they finished he asked again exactly where they had seen the blaze. He then checked the date on his calendar. It was the 30th of November. His face was ashen when he explained. The racing driver Graham Hill had crashed his Piper Aztec in that very field near Arkley golf course exactly twenty-five years earlier, on 29th November 1975, while attempting to land at Elstree in heavy fog. The crash and resulting explosion and fire killed all six members of the racing team on board.

This knowledge left everyone in the room with the uncanny feeling that they had been in contact with the world of spirits.

There were to be many other instances when our wizard was made aware of forces beyond the explainable but only two that affected him directly and personally.

⊷─◇─⊶

It was a perfectly ordinary day in the office. It had been a quiet morning and, as he was about to take out his lunch, he was surprised to hear the bell on the shop/warehouse door below. Moving to the head of the stairs, he saw two gypsy women standing inside the door carrying their baskets of lace and pegs. As he approached them, the elder woman, the mother, looked into his eyes and said, "You don't want to buy anything! You have troubles! We can 'see'! We are both seventh daughters of seventh daughters and we have the power". Bob was stunned. At the time he was experiencing a number of problems, with weighty decisions to be made imminently, both with his relationship and also his business. He had no idea that anyone else even guessed he faced these dilemmas. Always a private and cautious man, he would never have discussed these matters with even his closest friends. Before he could react, the elder gypsy's manner changed. Her eyes glazed, and she appeared as if in a trance. In a continuous monotone she related in horrifyingly accurate detail the problems he was facing. She was aware of his movements and even the minutiae of a recent business trip he had paid to the United States. As he became convinced that the woman was reading his very soul, she came out of her trance and her daughter took over. She now told Bob that the worrying time he was having with his business would soon be over. His company would continue to flourish. However, his marriage would end and it would be a long, hard road to recovery, but he would have a new relationship and that although there would be losses and it would take many years, eventually all would be well for him and he would find the happiness that he was seeking. He was still standing on the lower steps of the staircase, and as they spoke of his most intimate inner self, he felt weak and hung on to the bannister. When they finally stopped and asked if he would like to know more, he was so terrified he pushed a ten-pound note into their hands, a lot of money in 1988, thanked them and wished them a very 'Good Day!'

Six hours later, when he arrived home, he was still shaking from the experience and cannot explain to this day why, when he had never seen them before and never saw them again, they should have approached him at a time when he was so emotionally vulnerable, or how they managed to read so much intimate detail about his circumstances.

The second event was even more shattering and was indeed a life-changing experience, but this occurred nearly thirty years later and will be described in due course, when the time is right.

Chapter Seven

– SYNCHRONICITY –

While Bob was busy, in retirement, exploring the dowsing potential of Cyprus, back in England, Susy was moving on with her life. She had been married and was coping with a demanding and highly responsible job. She had little time, or inclination, to dwell on her earlier 'peculiar gifts'. But she was unsettled and restless. Although fully occupied, she was searching for another kind of life.

Some years earlier, she had found and loved the island of Cyprus as a holiday destination, visiting as often as she could afford, and getting to know its people and their culture. Now, she became aware of a yearning to spend time there and believed an unseen hand was drawing her back. Eventually, as pressures at home reached crisis point, she could no longer resist the call. She let her house, packed her bags and flew to Cyprus.

She had little idea what she would do when she arrived, but with the help of local friends she soon found a place to rent and some work.

Influenced by the subtle 'magic' of the island, she felt she could again acknowledge her former, now much enhanced, gifts. She could see people clearly in their characteristic colour, see their vibrant auras and, while totally unaware at the time of the scientific studies being pursued and their relevance, she began to 'hear' different colours and 'see' different pitches as colours. She would unexpectedly experience a strong presentiment about people just by looking at them and often felt that she was guided towards certain situations and away from others. She began using her pendulum to help her in decision-making.

She gradually gathered around her a group of similar-minded and gifted friends. Many used the pendulum in a variety of different ways, some for information, some for decision-making and some to contact spirits. There were spiritual and psychic healers among the group, with long-standing experience, confident in their powers, while others were still insecure and fearful of the powers they possessed. All were very conscious of the potential of the gifts they held and were anxious that these powers be utilised for the good of others, while at the same time aware that in the wrong hands they could damage or destroy. Surrounded by these sensitive and supportive friends, Susy thrived. During regular meetings, members of the group would share their understanding of, and experiences in, their areas of expertise. Fascinated by the potential scope of these powers, Susy began researching the work of adepts in her gifts and so explored other ways of using them. She became increasingly sensitive to the vibes around her. At times she was terrified by the intensity of her dreams, which she suspected and feared may be predictive.

In spite of having found a group of people who accepted her as 'normal' and respected and loved her for her special nature, she still felt she was searching. She had moved from one rented property to another for no apparent reason, except a feeling of restlessness and a sense that she had not yet found her 'home'. Then one day a friend told her of a bungalow for rent that sounded appropriate for her needs. She arranged to visit and, even as she approached the driveway, a tingling sensation told her that finally she had discovered what she was looking for. It was, indeed, a pretty property with a wonderfully sunny aspect and views of the mountains and the sea. But she knew that what she was feeling was far more deep-seated than the view. The interior was as congenial as she had expected, and she readily agreed the rent. As the property was already vacated she arranged to move in the following weekend.

(She has since recalled that she then returned to her existing house and wept. If questioned, she explains that after two years of searching she was finally quite convinced that she had found her 'home', and they were tears of relief and sheer joy.)

However, she was not fully aware at the time of the true importance of that decision. On further reflection, she firmly believes that she was 'guided' to the property, because it turned out to be an amazing, life-changing stroke of synchronicity. The property proved to have its own 'good aura', as it was built over strongly positive, earth energy lines, which will be discussed later. But even more than that, it belonged to our Wizard, Bob, and before long the two had forged a bond that made them a formidably powerful duo.

This is perhaps a good time to investigate further why Susy believes she is a witch and what evidence there may be to support her claim.

She had, for many years, been drawn to the ideas of natural healing, believing implicitly in the benefits of herbal remedies and controlled diet over the present-day urge to rush to the aid of pharmaceutical drugs.

She had been practising Reiki, the Japanese 'hands-on' or 'palm healing' technique, in which 'universal energy' is believed to be transferred through the palms of the practitioner to specific stress points in the body, to encourage both physical and spiritual healing.

She also studied and practised Reflexology in which the body is seen as a collection of individual organs and tissues which are connected to specific zones on the hands and feet. A disorder in a particular organ can be detected through manipulation of the associated zone in the foot. A high sensitivity to changes in that zone may enable the practitioner to determine the root of the disorder.

A long-time advocate of yoga, she fully understood the associated concepts of the power points of the body and the sites of the chakras. The word 'chakra' meaning a 'wheel' or 'circle' has an Indian origin and is used in Hinduism to mean the psychic energy centre of the body. The chakras are joined by energy channels or Nadi and represent the centres of balance in a body.

In all these skills, Susy found she was naturally proficient.

Being so highly tuned to all aspects of alternative medicine confirmed for her, more than ever, her mediaeval origins as a witch.

While the attitude to witchcraft, of both the civil authorities and the Church, in the Middle Ages, was ambivalent and tended to vacillate, the Church generally considered the claims of magic powers to be groundless. Witches were generally accepted merely as 'wise' women who claimed knowledge of herbal healing, which was often accompanied, for dramatic effect, by chants and spells. They invariably acted as midwives in rural communities, and as such were revered for assisting in the bringing forth of new life and were attributed with the skills of faith healing.

However, they were also often viewed with suspicion and because of their spells or 'hexes' were sometimes held responsible for a person's misfortunes. This made them vulnerable and although mediaeval executions were mainly for heresy, some witches were accused of working through Satan and hence were punished as heretics. Even in the Middle Ages there was a distinction made between 'white witches' who healed, even if by methods which we would today find grotesque and abhorrent; dispensed love potions; were adepts in astrology and alchemy but certainly intended no harm; and 'black witches' who claimed the ability to fly, levitate, escape from their bodies, dispense curses and worship the devil. All of these latter activities were believed to be aided by Satan.

While it is true that some witches were burnt at the stake during the twelfth and thirteenth centuries, it was not until the Renaissance and the fifteenth to eighteenth centuries that the Church, urged on by leading theologians of the day, began the great witch-hunts of history. Possibly the first recorded execution for witchcraft was Joan of Arc in 1431. However, after the publishing of Heinrich Kramer's book 'Malleus Maleficarum', which proclaimed the validity of witchcraft, and the pronouncements of Paracelsus and Martin Luther, the Church began to view witchcraft as a real threat and the seeds were set for mass slaughter. Between the years 1495 and 1531 fewer than a dozen witches were burned at the stake, but after John Calvin and his vigorous reformers arrived on the scene, more than 500 were executed in only two years (Wikipedia).

In the next 200 years more than 40,000 women were to die, while others suffered ostracism and abuse at the hands of fearful neighbours.

In his seminal work on witchcraft, Evans-Pritchard laid out his understanding of a witch's powers. He maintained that witchcraft was a power that some people possess naturally, an inborn property that they inherit. While generally they mean no harm, they have the ability to harm other human beings, animals or crops, without performing any special acts. They can cause damage by a look or a malicious thought, and sometimes may even do so involuntarily. His most important point was that 'witches are born' not made ('Witchcraft, Oracles and Magic among the Azande' Sir Edward Evans-Pritchard, 1937).

Susy feared that these two latter points may well apply to her.

These white witches, also called 'cunning folk' or 'blessing witches', worked mainly among ordinary country people who trusted the old, familiar folk-remedies and herbal lore. They accepted more readily that the world contained 'hidden forces' beyond their comprehension, than did their more sophisticated and educated town cousins. As the skills of witchcraft were associated with wisdom, the classical concept of the 'old crone' was born. Many of these 'ancients' had young acolytes or apprentices who at an early age were demonstrating the latent potential to succeed their mentors.

We have mentioned before that Susy was conscious at a very early age of being 'different' from her peer group. She readily acknowledges that her abilities are hereditary although she was aware of no evidence of this in her parents or immediate predecessors. However, she clearly remembers, as a tiny child, visits to a great grandmother whose life was veiled in mystery. Even as she grew older, she was never allowed to visit alone, even though the old lady lived in a house just down the street. She had what Susy now describes as a 'silent aura', and said very little. And yet this remarkable woman had lived an amazing life particularly for her times. Growing up during the early years of the twentieth century she saw the transition from the restrictive Victorians to the relatively wanton Edwardians. However, her rural farming background, one would expect, would have given her little opportunity to be more than a modest housewife, living within view of the house in which she was born. Yet, even as the First World War threatened to tear Europe apart, she travelled the world. No-one in the family seemed to know under what circumstances she visited the Far East or toured for months through South and Central America and no-one ever knew where her money came from. She ultimately returned to the place of her birth, where she settled and gave birth to Susy's maternal grandfather, leaving every aspect of her earlier adventures shrouded in mystery. If she did indeed carry psychic powers it is possible that she was drawn, against all the odds, towards areas of the world where these preternatural arts are more appreciated and practised. It is also likely, that as she grew older, she became more aware of the gifts that she had and was perhaps scared of their power, and so wrapped them away in a blanket of silence that ultimately engulfed her life.

Although still a small child, Susy was very conscious of a special feeling or 'presence' in the house. The focus of this seemed to be her great grandfather's clock. Whenever she looked at it she saw a clear vision of its departed owner. Remarkably this did not alarm her, and she appears to have found it quite normal. Throughout her childhood she accepted as natural her strong predictions of death and she did not find it in any way unusual that she always knew when people were about to die. She ran to break the news to her mother in advance of each of her great grandparents' deaths.

While a number of instances, during her teenage years and into her working life, strongly suggest witch-like qualities, she admits trying to deny these powers and believes, anyway, that they are diminished during adolescence due to the rise of hormones and attention to other interests. Similarly, once the energy is diverted into first, the working world or career, and then into home building and perhaps rearing children, the psychic powers are repressed. Certainly, for Susy, it was not until she broke free and moved to Cyprus that she felt the return of her earlier gifts. She left behind responsibilities of family and relationships and also shed the daily routine and stresses of her career. Magnified by the natural energies of the island and enhanced by contact with like-minded and similarly-gifted friends, she now experienced her powers growing exponentially. She began to see auras with greater intensity and feel the psychic energy fields around people as she met them. Her predictive dreams became more real and she became increasingly conscious of the immense responsibility such predictive information placed on her. If these dreams involved others that she knew, and the information she was receiving would affect their lives, was she to tell them or not? She understood that such information could work in different ways depending on the mental or emotional state of the person who received it. In some cases, it could prove extremely beneficial, enabling the receiver to take protective, evasive action. However, in other cases the knowledge might cause destructive emotional distress, pre-emptive or precipitous action that may ultimately prove destructive, or influence decision-making that could result in a self-fulfilling prophecy. The burden of disclosure weighed heavily on her.

Dreams, and even day-time flashes of inspiration, often brought less traumatic messages. Sometimes she would wake suddenly with a word or a name clearly imprinted in her mind. Although, usually, at the time they would seem meaningless, invariably before the day was out their significance would be revealed. This was a quirk she shared with the wizard.

One such insight involved Bob and was a time when he was researching his ancestral background. His paternal grandfather, in spite of being a senior government engineer, had enjoyed a 'lively' life. Having worked for many years in both South Africa and South America, he had managed, with great subterfuge, to conduct two quite independent lives. It was not until many years after his death that Bob's father discovered, through a surprise visit from Sao Paulo, that he had half siblings across the globe. As grandfather was ultimately reported 'drowned at sea' grandma had married again, but her earlier life, and background, always remained shrouded in mystery. Susy, anxious to help in the research, had delved deep into the reports held in the British Records Office archives. Soon she was buried under a welter of conflicting and increasingly confused paperwork. Then, one night, a name came to her clearly. 'Hetty'. Nowhere had that name been written and there was no indication where, if at all, it fitted into the research she was doing. The next day she casually said to Bob, "Who was Hetty?" His surprise was obvious. No-one had ever mentioned that name and yet it was the name by which his grandmother, Esther, was known within the family. While the disclosure of the name proved an uncanny revelation of Susy's rare ability, the ramifications of the family history were never satisfactorily unravelled. Never-the-less their joint findings produced an interesting scenario in Bob's subsequent Biography.

(Bob's major inspirational message came in a similar way. Again, he woke suddenly from a deep sleep with a name in his head. Now, those of you who know Bob will know he is 'bad with names'. The fact that he even remembered this one was remarkable. 'Bruce Cathie'. Bob vows he had never heard or seen the name before. As soon as he was out of bed he turned on his computer to Google the name. To his amazement, he found that Cathie was a New Zealand airline pilot who had written a number of books related to flying saucers and the 'world energy grid'. Fascinated by the similarity of Cathie's experiences and beliefs to his own, he contacted his cousin in New Zealand to see if Mike had heard of him. "Oh!" said Mike, "Bruce Cathie, everyone in New Zealand knows him." Bob would dearly have liked to learn more but sadly Cathie died in 2013 at the age of 83 and to this day Bob has no idea how or from where that name came to him.)

Susy also realised that not only dreams brought her visions of the past or future, but she sometimes had violent physical, empathetic reactions to a situation and this could often take the form of a sudden and intense pain which might indicate the circumstances in a situation that was being investigated. A crushing pain across her legs was to reveal a tragic accident with a farm cart, a crippling pain in her chest and her ultimate collapse was to confirm a death by heart attack and she has also suffered shooting and stabbing with an uncanny accuracy, enabling her to reveal the exact position of an inflicted wound.

She had formed a close attachment to a friend who had many years of experience in spiritual healing and was well practised in the skill of regression. Susy sought her help in an attempt to determine the source of her own powers. With the guidance of this friend she was gently encouraged to regress to her past lives. She recalls with great clarity two very different experiences.

She sees clearly a rocking horse in the corner of a room where there is also a small bed. She is in the nursery. She knows that it is her room. She is a little girl about five years old and it is a middle-class home at the turn of the 18th/19th century. She feels that she is loved and spoilt. She has before her a vivid image of her much-loved mother. She sees her high-waisted, empire line dress, much favoured in the time of Jane Austin. The fabric is a fine, blue muslin, embroidered with tiny daisies. The mother is seated at a mirror and Susy is brushing her mother's hair. She senses this is a privilege and she thrills at the feel of her mother's silky tresses as she strokes them.

The scene faded leaving Susy with a great sense of loss as she retains a strong, inner impression of every detail of the scene. Her guide then amazed her by describing the exact pattern and material of the mother's dress. She acknowledged that she too had been present in the scene and it is their belief that the guide had indeed been Susy's mother in that life and so it was unsurprising that they had felt an immediate attraction when they met.

Susy's second attempt to reveal her past brought a very different tableau. The time was earlier, probably very early 18th century and truly Dickensian in nature. She found herself in a filthy hovel where the stench was almost unbearable. In the corner was a small emaciated boy. She knew instantly she was looking at herself and the impression was so strong it resembled an out-of-body experience. The boy was shivering but lay curled up and clutching something in his hands. Looking closer, she recognised it as a lady's white lace handkerchief. The child was holding it as though it was the most precious thing he had ever seen. She felt his happiness in what he possessed. It had been some days earlier, the last time he had found the energy to scramble out of the shack to find food, when he had spotted the pretty lady drop the hanky on the street. He had picked it up and carried it home. It was the most delicate and beautiful thing he had ever seen, and he treasured it, both as a reminder of the pretty lady but also as a symbol of the wonderful life he believed others could live that he would never enjoy. Susy was still present when his energy was exhausted and his spirit finally left his wretched little body and she sobbed as she told the tale. She recalled feeling the pain as strongly as if she were experiencing her own death.

However, neither of these regressions gave her any indication that she had witchcraft in her history. She has no irrational fear of fire which suggests that she was not burned at the stake. However, there is one aspect of her present experience that she feels is unexpected and strange.

She is a strong swimmer and loves the sport but whether she is in the pool, the sea, or even just under the shower she has a totally irrational fear of having her head under water. Even when washing her hair, she cranes her head far back to avoid getting her face wet. If, by some misfortune, her head should sink beneath the water, she instantly experiences violent panic from which it takes her some time to recover.

She believes that this is a strong indicator that, if not acknowledged as a witch, she was seen in some earlier 'coming' as a herbal healer and perhaps was punished as a 'scold' or 'nagging wife' which would usually have meant the 'ducking stool'. She may never know!

Bob, however, was relying entirely on his rods at the time he met Susy. He had always considered his skills from the practical viewpoint and had not ventured into the psychic aspect of the powers he was tapping into.

While they had operated in different fields using different methods, they soon realised that their fundamental psychic skills were similar. They regularly shared experiences and the results of their research, and also began practising each other's methods. Susy soon became accomplished with the rods but Bob, although competent, never really felt as comfortable with the pendulum.

While still using her pendulum for preference, Susy tentatively sought to discover its scope. She had never used it to seek for lost items or for determining with mathematical precision. She knew that Bob could use his rods to distinguish between items and so she set out to practise. She had a collection of gemstones which she laid out in a row. Shuffling them unseen beneath a cloth she asked her pendulum to show her which was the ruby. As she moved the pendulum slowly down the line keeping it as still as possible, it initially stayed calm and vertical. Then with sudden movement it started to gyrate frantically. Peeping beneath the cloth she spied the ruby. Not convinced that this was anything but coincidence, she reshuffled and repeated several times and without fail the pendulum clearly indicated the precise position of the ruby. Finally, she was confident that she could use her pendulum to find items that were lost.

As the witch and wizard worked together they became aware that their psychic energy was increased but even then, they still had little idea, in those early days, of the scope and variety of energy sources that their skills would lead them into.

Chapter Eight

– EARTH ENERGY –
AND AN
ENERGY CROSSROADS

The first thing they discovered, as they talked to friends about their experiences, was the tremendous interest so many people had in the subject. They had always believed that most people were in denial, or, at best, doubters, but they soon realised that this was not necessarily the case.

They were each to find, as they travelled around, that as soon as the rods appeared they would have a circle of interested observers. On a visit to the ancient archaeological site, Gobeklitepe, in eastern Turkey, they found they were surrounded by a curious group of Turkish tourists, all anxious to 'have a go'. They were highly amused when an elderly lady totally hidden behind a full burka grabbed the rods and started walking slowly and seriously towards an ancient ceremonial altar where pre-pubescent girls had been sacrificed to the gods as vestal virgins.

In another area around stone cleansing-pools a party of very jolly university professors from Istanbul joined in the search for more detailed historical information.

Similar interest from another group of scientists and engineers was witnessed when the ancient site of Vouni, in Cyprus, was being investigated.

On a trip to Iran, Bob was anxious to explore the hidden depths of ancient Persia but was, perhaps understandably, a little nervous of exhibiting his skills. However, after the first few days he could resist it no longer and threw caution to the wind.

While he was dowsing a powerful portal in the forecourt of the Jameh Mosque in Esfahan, he was again conscious of the intrigued interest of the many tourists of all nationalities. He was, however, aware that the Iranians, Turks and other eastern cultures accepted what he was doing as quite natural and those that took the rods from him were all competent dowsers. It was obvious that the entire concept is an intrinsic part of their culture and psyche.

Meanwhile, back at home the general interest was such that it was decided to set up a basic dowsing course for complete beginners. Both Susy and Bob were overwhelmed by the response and found that they immediately had to arrange a second course. In truth, some of the interest had been originally inspired by Bob's talk to the Anglo-Turkish Association, but the interest grew like Topsy. Those that had been on the beginners' courses told their friends, who clamoured for places on the 'next' course, while those that felt they had graduated, demanded guidance into more advanced experiences.

For their earliest courses they chose the Baspinar Plateau, an area of flat land amid the Kyrenia mountain range, which runs west to east parallel to the north coast of Cyprus. Both our witch and wizard had explored this area before and knew that it held hidden secrets that would be readily yielded up to even the most inexperienced dowser. They knew their followers could not fail to be impressed.

Before the features of the area are discussed it is important that more is learnt about the energy that is being investigated.

It will already be apparent that the forces being tapped into are ubiquitous, and although there is much research, there is still no definitive explanation for their source or strength.

As Bob's experiences took him into different spheres, he had begun to read widely into all aspects of dowsing and, inevitably in his travels, was drawn to other dowsers, who shared their own experiences.

He was surprised and, perhaps, a little flattered to be approached by another highly experienced dowser. She was, at the time, doing much the same as him, and had been employed to locate water for a well. She had found two streams running through the property but was not confident in determining which had the greater flow and, thereby, the optimum siting for the well. Bob was happy to work with her and together they confirmed the best location. The client was satisfied, and the two dowsers became friends.

It transpired that his new friend Layle was extremely knowledgeable about earth energy and ley lines, and she introduced Bob to a completely new aspect of his skill.

Up to that point Bob had been mainly concerned with the energy field produced by running water. He was already aware that even moving streams can produce more than one type of energy field. Some he found were positive and harmless, whereas other underground streams produced a negative field that is in conflict with the natural earth field and is considered to be a form of 'energetic pollution'. These streams are called 'Black-streams' or 'Black-water' and can form what is known as geopathic or telluric stress. These could have serious effects on those living above them, as our witch and wizard were to learn later when they encountered people with health and emotional problems.

Under Layle's guidance, Bob quickly came to recognise the difference between the rods' response to the energy fields produced by water and the energy field detected due to the natural earth energy fields or ley lines.

Cyprus is a very 'special' island for many reasons. It has a long and rich history, due largely to its location at the eastern end of the Mediterranean, nestling in a sheltered cove, north of Egypt, south of Turkey and west of the Levant. It proved the perfect provisioning post for voyagers in earlier times, not least, the Crusaders.

It is a pleasant, fertile land with an interesting geological structure. It is also highly energetic and is criss-crossed by powerful ley lines.

It is now believed that the entire globe is encircled by a naturally occurring, three-dimensional electromagnetic network or grid. Within this grid there are especially powerful forces or 'ley lines', a term coined by Alfred Watkins in 1925. But these lines had been known, and their power exploited, long before that. They are the 'Dragon' lines of ancient Chinese culture. They can be located and identified by highly sensitive electromagnetic meters, but also by dowsers.

These lines have been the subject of numerous extensive studies world-wide, and there have been some remarkable findings.

Hamish Miller, a dowsing authority in the UK, spent two years, with his friend and chronicler, Paul Broadhurst, investigating the St Michael and Mary Lines from St Michael's Mount in Cornwall diagonally across the country to their end in Norfolk. Using only dowsing rods they plotted these powerful lines, recording variations in their paths and noting the remarkable number of historic sites falling directly on the lines, not least, Stonehenge, Avebury, Silbury Hill and many others. They published their account of the journey as 'The Sun and the Serpent', which makes a fascinating and most convincing read.

It is now generally acknowledged that all ancient places of worship and other buildings of great significance in a community, from the Taj Mahal to the Pyramids of Egypt, from Machu Picchu to the Mayan Pyramids, the Vatican to the Pentagon, were all sited on ley lines, and also have a distinctive alignment with the stars. Star alignment and solar- and lunar-activity are now believed to have a direct effect on the earth's geomagnetism, and so ancient civilisations appear to have been aware of this and able to make the necessary calculations to ensure a positive result.

Cathedrals and churches, mosques and temples have been built, not only on ley lines but many are on sites that were used by much earlier inhabitants for worship and sacrifice. This suggests, again, that very primitive communities were aware of the presence and the power of these forces and had the ability to locate them.

It is now understood that, so great is the Chinese respect for the power of these Dragon lines, all great Chinese leaders and dignitaries are obliged to build their properties on the positive energy lines which will endow them with good 'chi', or positive life force.

Layle, who was well versed in the power of earth energy and had worked extensively on aspects of Feng Shui and the positive effects on health of alignment and balance, was happy to share her experiences. It was with her guidance that our witch and wizard discovered the mysteries of the Baspinar Plateau.

The first time he visited, even Bob was amazed at the strength of the forces. The entire plateau is traversed by clearly defined earth energy lines. These can be marked out and readily identified as positive or negative, alternately, with the energy channels being as wide as three metres. The grid-formation is clearly defined.

Although Bob had read of the grid, and the work being done in England by dowsers from Bristol to map the grid across their area, he had never seen such distinct evidence of the pattern. He was to see it again on numerous occasions. The grid was used by the early builders of the gymnasium at the late Bronze Age site of Salamis, to align the massive columns. The energy lines can be readily detected by the rods passing between the columns. Similarly, when dowsing in the ancient site of Taxien, just outside Valletta in Malta, it was clear that the early builders had knowledge of the location of the earth energy lines when siting the structures.

Back on the Baspinar Plateau and moving slowly across the central flat area, ten broad energy lines can be detected running west to east, while eight travel north to south or south to north, at approximately right angles to them. So powerful and regular are these lines that walking down one central path of the plateau with the rods held high above the head there are so many crossing forces that the rods swing freely in circles, totally out of the control of the dowser. If the dowsers walked the path slowly, the rods would respond to the lines, which were consistently approximately 3 metres apart, by moving in very precise directions regardless of the normal 'yes' or 'no' direction of the rods. An observer would note both rods moving to the right, then, on the next line, both to the left, then one to the right or left etc. Even when the novice dowsers were blind-folded and instructed to walk slowly along the path, the rods would respond in exactly the same way at the same point. Everyone was totally astounded yet totally convinced.

This then proved an ideal site for the first courses for 'would-be' dowsers. While normally successful dowsing demands a degree of belief and self-confidence, the power on the plateau was so great that everyone, even the most doubtful and faint-hearted, felt an immediate response in their rods and became excited and eager to move on.

Further investigation by Bob and Susy revealed that overlaying and crossing the normal earth-energy grid were a number of stronger ley lines. In this particular location they tended to run diagonally to the grid. Always anxious to use a scientific approach and wherever possible work separately and check each other's results, they took it in turns to plot the direction of the lines, their source and end, reporting the findings to an independent scribe. The accuracy of their results when cross-checked was astounding. They confirmed that there were three ley lines crossing the plateau. One line travelled generally in a west to east direction and careful questioning of the rods indicated that it ended somewhere in Syria. More detailed research may ultimately indicate the exact location of its source and destination.

The other two lines proved most interesting and by strange coincidence both our witch and wizard were to encounter these again in completely different circumstances, one in another country and the other on a different continent.

The next line they discovered travelled in a north-westerly direction towards Italy. Using eliminating questioning of the rods, they revealed that it passed through the Vatican and became known to them as the 'Vatican' line. Following their normal procedure, they then checked the polarity of the line and were not a little surprised to find that it was strongly negative. (This revelation did leave them wondering if it was the influence of this ley line that was, at least in part, responsible for some of the more brutal and negative behaviour emanating from the Vatican throughout history; the Crusades; the excesses of the Borgias; the Inquisition.)

Some years later Susy was to visit Rome. In great trepidation she stood outside the Vatican and mentally tuned herself to do what she had come to do. She readily located the ley line and confirmed that it was the negative line they had identified on the Baspinar Plateau. Then, with an enormous surge of her extra-ordinary mental power she moved it. There was no earthquake, no thunder, no freak streak of lightning, no change to the naked eye, but when she viewed the photograph that she had taken she knew she had been successful. A white streak, or energy sprite, appeared on the digital picture at exactly the point where she had removed the line and careful examination of the picture showed a faint white line passing from behind St Paul's directly to the spire of a church in the distance.

The third line they discovered was to be the most revealing. It travelled roughly diagonally across the plateau in a north-west/south-easterly direction. As it appeared heading for Egypt, it was no surprise when the rods confirmed that it passed through the Giza pyramids. Using the rods, they turned north, and followed the line on an amazing odyssey. Travelling up through Greece and into the Balkan states, they confirmed that the line passed through the recently discovered Bosnian Pyramids. Susy was to visit these at a later date and was able to confirm the presence of this line in the powerfully energetic area of the pyramids. The line then swung westerly across Europe and on into England, passing through Stonehenge and other ancient features. It crossed Ireland and out into the Atlantic, reaching land again under Newfoundland. Veering south-west it travelled through Nova Scotia, where Bob identified it later. Turning further south it moved down the eastern seaboard of the United States under the White House and the Pentagon and ever southward through the Mayan Pyramid. Their excitement at this initial discovery can hardly be imagined. Subsequent research has shown that this is a well-known and documented ley line but for our witch and wizard it is something personal and very special and will be a subject of interest and further research for many years to come.

The Plateau became a regular site for their dowsing courses and, as this necessitated constant checking of the energy lines, it soon became apparent that while maintaining their general position, these lines are influenced by extra-terrestrial effects such as phases of the moon and changes in solar activity, like sun-spots. It is believed that the oscillation may be as much as a metre back and forth, but the extent will depend on the intensity of the external influences and the latitude of the location. It has also been observed that the strength of the field varies throughout the day. It would appear that the sun pushes the energy ahead of it as a particular field is at maximum energy approximately one hour before sunrise and then gradually deteriorates until it is at its weakest in the evening.

Once the dowsers were familiar with the concept of earth energy, the plateau offered other areas of investigation and interest. Taking a narrow pathway from the plateau to the west, a group would be led into the surrounding rocky woodland. Here, they would enter another world, a world of the ancient and deeply spiritual and they were about to discover a completely different aspect of dowsing. As they approached the shady glade, some people immediately declared a reluctance to enter the area, while others began to complain of feeling nauseous or headachy. Some had difficulty breathing and found the atmosphere unusually heavy and oppressive. They were entering an area of very powerful earth energy, both positive and negative. It would seem that the rocks themselves were emanating strong electromagnetic fields. These had been detected by very early civilisations and the area had been deemed sacred, and folklore and the rods suggested that the ancient gods still inhabit the area. All dowsers passing down the narrow path were advised to ask permission, through their rods, to enter. There were two huge overhanging rocks that appeared to have a primitive human form. They epitomised humanity and fertility. Below these symbolic stones were a group of flat rocks that appeared to have been an altar. These were very negative, and many dowsers showed a natural reluctance to approach them. The intensity of the negative forces strongly suggested that this had been an area of sacrifice to the gods. Consequent questioning of the rods confirmed that it had indeed been an area of human sacrifice.

Nearby, however, there is a rock that has the appearance of a seat. This is on a positive energy line and all who sat in it acknowledged a great feeling of well-being and peace.

No-one entering this very special, sheltered vale failed to be overawed by the powerful presence of the supernatural. All were left questioning their own beliefs and whether they were feeling the touch of the ancient gods or were being stroked by the hand of Mother Nature, Kybele, herself.

On the eastern side of the plateau dowsers were introduced to yet another aspect of the dowsing experience. Here, there is a collection of stones that appear to have been an ancient altar. But the rods show that this was placed strategically on a junction of energy lines. This dramatically increases the energy at that spot and it is known as a 'portal'. At these points, not only the lines from the earth grid but also other energy lines cross. The power of the portal depends on the number and strength of the energy lines crossing. The intense energy at the centre of the portal can be identified as either positive or negative and will spiral clockwise or anticlockwise, upwards to the sky or down into the earth. While the rods will unerringly detect all these features, Susy will always use her pendulum which demonstrates clearly the rotation of the forces.

In a later section we will discover how some of these portals, when positive, can be used to restore health.

The mentors chose an energetically quiet area on the western side of the plateau to demonstrate yet another aspect of their expertise. They explained that while the great electromagnetic fields of nature were difficult to manipulate, it was possible to create and destroy other energy fields.

Quantum physics has shown that all matter, at its sub-atomic core, is in constant motion and actually constitutes energy. This includes every living cell, inanimate objects and particles in space. Countless studies have shown that in its seemingly solid form, matter also emits energy and it is from this source the world's electromagnetic grid emanates. However, not all electromagnetic fields are of this magnitude. Even minute changes or distortions of the normal earth 'state' can produce a magnetic change that can be detected by sensitive dowsers. In a similar way to an army marching across a bridge and setting up a vibration or sympathetic resonance that could destroy the bridge, so with simple regular actions dowsers can cause a rhythmic disturbance that can be registered by the rods.

The area chosen was first checked with the rods and the absence of energy lines in the immediate area was confirmed. Arranging the dozen, or so, course members in a ring on their knees, the leaders instructed them to pick up a stone. They were then shown how to tap the stone firmly on the ground. On the seventh stroke the next person would start tapping seven. All would continue tapping until the circle was complete. The participants watched their rods with amazement when, as they checked the circle for the presence of energy, there was a clear indication of the presence of a circular energy line in the exact position of the tapping. While the witch and wizard both knew that this created energy line would last in that spot indefinitely, they were anxious not to leave a disturbance in the natural energy of the area and so proceeded to show the, still mesmerised, course members how to remove the energy line they had created. This was achieved by gently rubbing the hand over the area that had been tapped and wishing the energy dispersed. After a moment or two the rods confirmed that the energy line had disappeared. This observation amazed the members of the group.

While some, already challenged by the concept of telluric energy itself, found this last display almost beyond credibility, others found it exciting and exhilarating and vowed to study further.

Everyone left the plateau exhausted but intellectually and emotionally challenged and full of wonder.

The creation of an energy circle is not a new phenomenon. For thousands of years ancient religious cultures have been aware of the possibility of enhancing energy by ritual chanting and dance (sound, which is a particle distortion and dance, a co-ordinated rhythmic movement). One very visual example is seen at the Moslem Hajj. Here, thousands of pilgrims from all over the world congregate to process around the Ka'bah, believed by followers of Islam to be the most sacred spot on earth. As the faithful rotate in an anticlockwise direction, the seven circuits of Tawaf, keeping the Ka'bah on their left, they chant prayers of supplication. Similarly, the Jews, at major festivals, can be seen encircling seven times the Old Temple on Temple Mount. This ritual is believed to increase the positive aura, or energy in the area. In some cases, this can be so great that it can produce emotional hysteria, even orgasmic experiences.

As the number of their followers grew, Bob and Susy spent time searching for new and exciting places to direct their interest and investigation. They sought out ancient historical sites and found that they were able to enhance and extend the information that had already been made available by archaeologists and historians. In numerous cases they discovered that many of the sites recorded had been inhabited by earlier dwellers. They also found that they could discover more about the lives and times of these peoples. They realised that by checking areas themselves first and then producing a questionnaire on which their course members recorded their rods' answers, a detailed consensus of facts could be compiled. They strictly insisted that there should be no collusion so that all the answers could be accepted as independent results.

One of the earliest areas then chosen was on the north coast of Cyprus below the Baspinar Plateau. The submerged fish ponds and the nearby area of Sardunya is well documented, and as the history is long and extensive, our witch and wizard believed that it would be a good area to investigate and perhaps challenge accepted theories. Their initial decision was confirmed when they heard that local folklore cited the area as one of the possible locations for the 'mythical' Atlantis ('Through the Third Eye' by Olcay Akdeniz).

But, before they had the opportunity to organise another group dowse, the demand for their skill was diverted to answer a call which carried them into another aspect of their art.

Chapter Nine

– CRIES FOR HELP –

It was on one of the beginners' courses on Baspinar Plateau, as they walked in the mountains from one site to another, chatting as they went, that one of the young women remarked casually that she felt her illness and constant feeling of general debility could be the result of negative earth energy. She and her husband had, for many years, been working hard, building the home of their dreams. But their plans seemed to have been constantly thwarted and they were finding it difficult to complete the project. Throughout this period, she had not enjoyed good health and was both physically and emotionally weak. By the time she met Bob, she was almost at her wits' end.

Although they were, at the time, some ten miles from her home, which Bob had never seen, he was most anxious to help her. He decided there and then to try out, for the first time, his ability to 'remote view'. She pointed across the mountains in the direction of her home. He held her hand and closed his eyes. Delving deeply into his subconscious, he sought the location with his 'third eye'. Psychically arriving at his destination, he was jolted back to consciousness by the strength of the negativity he felt. The cause was two powerful underground streams of 'black-water', formed when the path of negative earth energy aligns with a deep and powerfully flowing water course. Together these radiate intensely negative electromagnetic fields, and in this instance, they flowed directly under the property. Realising instantly that it was this negative radiation that was contributing to the health problems, he offered to visit the house to investigate further. He believed that the only possible remedy may be to move the offending field. However, he was very conscious that he was not capable of effecting this action and was not even confident that his long-distance dowsing had been accurate. He badly needed the support of his witch.

He eagerly awaited the return of Susy from the UK, and together they accepted an invitation to lunch. Even as they approached the house, Susy felt nauseous. She was conscious of a strong, all-pervading smell of gas, although there was no gas supply on the property and no evidence of the source of the odour. She discovered later that this was common in these circumstances. She found it incredibly difficult to overcome her feelings of revulsion and so enter the property, to enjoy the warm hospitality offered.

Together, the two more than doubled their individual powers, and they set to work confidently to confirm the black-water that Bob had previously identified. Although concerned for the well-being of the house-holders, Bob was quietly excited to find that his remote viewing experiment had worked. The negativity seemed to permeate the whole house. The only possibility of real relief was to move the lines. However, this was a difficult task and neither Bob nor Susy had experience of the procedure at that stage. There are numerous considerations to be taken into account, not least the risk of moving the energy into the path of another property. It is not yet known if the change in direction is, in fact, permanent, or whether over time nature will re-adjust the energy field. It is extremely energy-draining for the dowser who attempts it, and even experienced dowsers will only perform the exercise as a last resort. Dismissing the possibility of moving the lines, they sought other ways of helping minimise the effect. They turned to the principles of Feng Shui. They carefully checked the direction of the negative flow through the property and discovered that the master bedroom was directly above the most powerful stream. They immediately recommended that this room was abandoned, at least committed to the intermittent, short term use as a guest room, and that the room furthest from the stream be used as the main bedroom. The bed was turned so that the head was as far as possible from the offending field. They then found that the other stream passed through the lounge again directly beneath the settee on which the couple usually sat to watch TV. The room was suitably re-arranged with the settee as far as possible from the source of the problem.

By the time the witch and the wizard left the house, the owners were already feeling more positive and optimistic for the future.

Subsequent checks proved a dramatic improvement in the health and general well-being of the occupants and Bob and Susy were set fair on another path to test their skills.

News of such events passed like a forest fire through the social groups of the island. Soon both Bob and Susy were receiving calls from people who were experiencing health and emotional problems and suspected these may be caused by unseen elements in their properties. They realised that the time was approaching when they would encounter a situation in which there would be no alternative to moving the lines. They therefore set about practising this demanding skill. They took themselves off to a remote headland and dowsed until they discovered an errant energy line. They checked carefully and noted its track. Then, using their combined psychic energy, they willed it to move. There was no visual change in their surroundings but when they checked with the rods, the line had indeed moved on to a new track. Encouraged by this early success they found another line and sent it into the sea. When they were confident that they could achieve this move independently, they returned home satisfied but totally exhausted.

They were also confident by this time that they could 'cut' the energy lines and so prevent negative energy from entering a property. They practised together, with deep mental focus and a co-ordinated series of tappings with their staffs over a known energy line. Subsequent checks with the rods showed that the negative flow had been halted. Anxious not to alter the natural electromagnetic fields unnecessarily they retraced the procedure and replaced the flow.

Our wizard had little idea at that time how useful he was to find this ability.

It was some months later and he was touring in beautiful Costa Rica. He had travelled from the far south-western extremity of the country, enjoying the exotic scenery, the wilderness treks, Pacific Ocean snorkelling, and precarious walks over the tropical forests on the hanging bridges, when he arrived at the base of one of the major volcanoes. He was booked into a charming hotel which afforded fantastic views of the volcano about 5km away. Entering his delightfully appointed chalet in the late afternoon and tired after a hot, sunny day travelling, he flopped down onto one of the two large double beds in the room. He immediately felt indescribably ill. He felt sick and was suddenly seized by a violent stomach pain. At first, he feared he had appendicitis or had been poisoned. Then, glancing through the window he saw the volcano. His acute awareness of earth energy alerted him, and he wondered if his condition was in some way related to the volcano. He staggered from the bed and instantly the pain was somewhat eased. He retrieved his rods from his rucksack. Checking the room, he found that an extremely powerful black-water energy line flowed in a straight line from the volcano directly under the bed. He went outside and confirmed the track of the energy. Summoning all his psychic strength he 'cut' the energy line. The rods confirmed that the powerful flow had been halted just outside the chalet. His pain and nausea miraculously vanished, and he enjoyed two good nights' sleep. However, on testing the area again before leaving, the rods showed that the energy was creeping back along its original path and he could only hope that the next occupant of the chalet was considerably less sensitive to the effects of geopathic stress.

It was not long before a friend approached both Bob and Susy with a problem in her property, very like the earlier one recorded. The house had been long in the building and every difficulty and hold-up had been encountered. The owners were seriously beginning to believe that the property was jinxed. Eventually, both began to suffer unexpected illnesses. The dowsers moved in with the rods and quickly identified two negative energy lines. One passed under the house directly beneath the master bedroom, the other very powerful line travelled slightly to the east of the house but close enough to exert a considerable influence on the occupants over a period of time. Initially, Bob and Susy again employed basic Feng Shui techniques, suggesting an abandonment of the master bedroom in favour of another room at the far end of the house. While this certainly improved the situation, Susy returned later, with her new-found skill, and diverted the energy, so that, while it maintained its original line and could not interfere with other property, it kinked around the house and passed it on the western boundary. The beneficial effect on the owner was immediate and while the established medical problems still had to be dealt with, her emotional strength increased, and she was infinitely more prepared to cope with the situation she was in.

Subsequent experience showed that invariably when a property appears to be jinxed, a negative energy line is present. Reflection suggests that the observed effects are not actually witchcraft or voodoo but the presence of the negative energy field which disturbs and destabilises the biorhythms of the occupants, and also, even workmen that are on site for any length of time. This in turn can affect decision-making and relationships, which may lead eventually to problems in the smooth completion of the project.

Our witch and wizard were to come across many such cases, where negative energy lines played at least some part in emotional problems. Fascinated by their findings, they began to look further into examples of negative fields affecting human physiology.

Many readers will remember the health-scare in Cornwall when radio-active radon gas was discovered to be escaping from the radium found in the underlying bedrock. Surveys at the time provided no hard evidence of a link with cancer, and the investigation died, leaving the inhabitants with their own uneasy doubts. Today radiation is acknowledged as one of the most significant causes of cancer.

Other countries have been more vigorous in their statistical data than the UK. Dr J Picard, in Moulins, France, noted an unusually large number of cancer cases in a confined area of the town. On dowsing, he discovered that all the cases were lying on, or close to, underground water veins that were emitting high doses of noxious radiation. Fearful of reprisals from a prejudiced medical profession, he did not publish his results. However, in 1973, Dr Dieter Aschoff, impressed by Picard's work, did publish a booklet, 'Can Official Science still deny the theory that cancer can be caused by stimulation zones?' In this he revealed that as far back as 1960 he had been advising his patients to have dowsers check for any negative forms of energy fields under areas where they spent extended periods of time. (Ref. 'The Divining Hand' by Christopher Bird.)

It is believed that now, some 60 years later, there are areas in Germany where systematic dowsing is done before residential building permits are granted and there is a widespread call for such surveys to become mandatory.

While the link between negative forms of earth energy and cancer has never been formally acknowledged there is abundant speculative evidence that various forms of radiation can have a deleterious effect on the human body. While some forms of radiation can be used to kill cancer cells, as in radio-therapy, there are other forms, that promote growth. It does not take a great leap in imagination to speculate that uncontrolled radiation could, in certain conditions, stimulate the abnormal growth of cells in the body, thus producing tumours or conversely inadvertently kill off healthy cells producing pernicious deficiencies.

Bob experienced a very personal demonstration of the effect of earth radiation from a totally unexpected quarter. Always being an enthusiastic gardener, he took great pride in the quality of his citrus crop when he settled in Cyprus. It was often remarked, with some slight exaggeration, that his limes were the size of lemons, lemons of oranges, oranges of grapefruit and grapefruit of footballs! It was therefore, with some disdain, he received the challenge of a neighbour who declared that she had larger lemons than he could imagine. With some degree of disbelief, he visited to view, and sure enough the lemons presented were enormous, nearly twice the size of Bob's best exhibit, with unusually knobbly peel. Barely believing his own eyes he photographed one of the monsters beside his prize specimen to record the difference for posterity. He then went in search of the tree that had produced these whoppers. He found it at a distance from the house and still bearing a few outsized fruit. This, he realised, was a job for the rods! He soon ascertained that the tree stood over a powerful negative, black-water flow. Convinced that this was the cause of the abnormality in the fruit, he tracked the black-water stream and as he had expected he found another tree some 100 yards away, producing similar distorted lemons. By this time Bob had sufficient circumstantial evidence of the electromagnetic, radiation effects of black-water, to be confident that this was indeed the seat of the problem. He advised his neighbour to avoid using the lemons and closed the case.

However, some months later when the scribe was thumbing through the dowsers' bible, Christopher Bird's 'The Divining Hand', she came upon a photograph of two lemons identical to the picture that Bob had taken a few months earlier. Thinking at first she was 'seeing things' she read on. The distorted lemon in the picture had all the features of the neighbour's lemon. It was the same size in relation to the 'normal' lemon beside it. It also had the uneven bobbled surface. The way it had been produced was elucidating. A scientist, in Germany, experimenting with the effect of radiation on cell growth and eradiated the roots of the lemon plant with ultra-sound. The plant had appeared to continue to grow normally but then had produced these massive and disfigured fruits. As his experiments were conducted in the laboratory in conjunction with the proper controls, it would appear that there was clear indication that certain forms of radiation promoted excessive cell growth. The wizard was delighted to hear this, as he observed, "If ultra-sound, why not black-water?"

Bob then realised that he had personally experienced this effect some years earlier. He had been walking through woodland one summer afternoon, when he noticed that amid the haphazard growth one straight row of taller, healthier trees stood out. The rods immediately confirmed a positive energy line following the exact path of the trees. On his return home, he was busy in his own woods, felling trees at the edge of his property, when he became aware of the reverse of what he had previously witnessed. There was a distinctive pattern of gnarled and ailing trees, surrounded by young trees with lush and healthy growth. Investigation with the rods showed that the dying trees were on a negative energy line.

It was only much later when he realised that the negative energy line, while a good distance from his own property, travelled diagonally across his woods and into his neighbour's property. Careful tracking showed the path to pass directly through the neighbour's house. He did not want to consider that this negative field may have contributed to the cancers that unexpectedly developed in both the original owner and subsequent owners of that beautiful home.

The next cry for help came from an unexpected quarter and carried them into yet another dimension. A close friend shared her concerns about the situation of a young acquaintance of hers. Since Brenda arrived on the island and had moved in with Turkish Cypriot friends, her previously successful company had begun a mysterious downhill slide and her health had deteriorated. She couldn't sleep and was highly stressed. When her psychic support team arrived, she was obviously on the verge of a nervous breakdown, weakly smiling a greeting, as tears streamed down her cheeks. Susy talked to her gently and Bob set to work with the rods. While a cup of coffee was being brewed, Susy followed Bob around the house. They met up for coffee and compared their initial findings. They immediately agreed that there was strong negative energy running under the bedroom but because the property was surrounded closely by other dwellings, moving it was not an option. Another bedroom was chosen, and the usual Feng Shui principles were employed. However, they were both convinced that the problem was more complex and deep rooted. Leaving their scribe in the sitting room they took off in opposite directions, in order to produce independent findings. Susy went in to the garden, while Bob remained in the sitting room. Even in this room, well away from the negative energy line, he was conscious of bad vibes. His rods immediately drew him to one corner of the room and he was soon passing information fast and furiously to his fascinated recorder. As he left the room through the patio window, Susy entered from the kitchen. Her instinct took her directly to the same corner of the room, where, like Bob, she began relating the results of her questioning of the rods. The similarity of the findings was astounding. They had both identified an unnatural death at that precise location. A young man of 28/29 years old had been stabbed in an altercation and had died. The year was 1966/67, in the midst of a troubled period for the people of the island. At the time there was no house on the land and it was assumed that it had been an olive grove.

Still not satisfied that the area had yielded up all its secrets, Susy had investigated the garden and found the spirit energy of a woman who had also met a violent death. The rods confirmed that this was the mother of the young man. Bob subsequently confirmed this.

Susy then exercised her fast-developing psychic powers to communicate with both the mother and the son. She ascertained that the spirit of the son was reluctant to leave the area as he knew his mother's spirit also lingered there. Like the many Turkish Cypriots who had suffered in the south of the island, so these two appeared to be Greek Cypriots who had become victims of the troubled north. Anxious to put the spirits at rest and relieve the property of the stress, and, realising that the spirits may remain vengeful over their plight, Susy returned to the son and assured him that although the property was inhabited by Turkish Cypriots, they felt no animosity towards their Greek neighbours and appealed to him to leave the property. She then spoke in a similar vein to the spirit of the mother appealing, on behalf of Brenda, for peace.

She waited for a moment, then, with tears of emotion, she tested the area with the rods for the presence of spirits. There were none.

They called Brenda, who was instantly aware of a change in aura, and flung her arms round Susy in gratitude and relief. Only then did she share with them the extraordinary information that her dog would never move near the particular corner of the living room, and when obliged to pass it on his path from the kitchen, he would never do so without whining and shrinking away. (This sensitivity of animals to the presence of extra-sensory vibes is very common and has regularly been encountered by the dowsers.)

Some months later, Susy was to meet with Brenda unexpectedly, at a party. At first, she did not recognise the glowing, confident girl that greeted her. She had taken up her life again and was very much 'back on track'.

One day while out walking, a friend, who knew of their exploits, was telling Bob that she believed that she had energy lines passing through her property and wondered if he and Susy could identify them. When asked why she thought this she remarked that she had not been sleeping particularly well, but also, she had noticed that there was one area of her hallway where her cats always appeared agitated to the extent that they had scratched the carpet bare at that point.

And so, armed with their rods, they descended on the property. Again, they easily confirmed each other's findings. The house was, indeed, on an energy line crossroads but all was not bad. While there was a negative line travelling along the hallway and through a section of the kitchen and another that ran diagonally across the driveway, there were positive lines that ran parallel to the driveway line through her sitting room, directly under her television chair. In this case they decided that no harm could be done by moving the offending negative line, and so they combined their psychic energy and gently eased the line from its position until it was safely outside the property. The owner declared that the result was like having her house exorcised and she immediately felt the atmosphere generally more congenial, she felt more relaxed, was sleeping better and the cats abandoned the threadbare carpet and have not been seen scratching in the house since.

Not all pleas for help are related to health or even the presence of adverse earth energy. Occasionally there is a rather different request and these instances, while vexing at the time, may not be serious and can provide quite amusing scenarios. However, the end results are not always as positive as were hoped.

Bob and Jen had been out for lunch with friends. The group had been specially assembled for their interest in dowsing as the hostess was hoping that Bob would be able to demonstrate his skills and tell her more about an ancient stone trough that was inset into the outer wall of her property. After lunch everyone left the house to watch the investigation. The hostess meticulously locked her front door.

Shortly after returning to the house, the party broke up and everyone made for their cars. On their way home Bob decided to stop at the DVD shop and acquire the evening's entertainment. To her horror, Jen found that her purse was missing from her bag. She knew that she had it when they had arrived in town as she had paid the car park attendant, and so they returned to their parking spot. Of course, there was no sign of a purse, the attendant had not seen one and more convincingly the rods showed that no purse had dropped on the ground in that area. Depressed, they returned home.

The next morning, they reported the loss to the police and, not unexpectedly, no purse had been handed in. There was very little money in the purse, but the value of the loss was in the purse itself and the credit cards and driving licences that it held. The rest of the day was spent cancelling and re-ordering credit cards and applying for replacement driving licences. But Jen could not settle. She felt stupid but was sure that she had not been careless. She would not just have 'dropped' something so precious. Then she had a thought. She phoned her 'help' line. Susy immediately agreed to return to the property and check with the rods. Jen then phoned the hostess who was full of remorse, and, sympathetic to the action of the rods, welcomed their return. She admitted that this was not the first time that this had happened and that she had regularly lost small items that could be easily sold. She said that she had harboured suspicions about the activities in the adjoining property and had even voiced them to the police but until the thieves were caught in the act there was little that could be done. But Susy was not finished. She felt a strong response from the purse and decided to track its path from the house. They must have made a comical picture as the three of them trailed through the gate on to the lane, Susy in front, confidently led by her rods, with Jen close on her tail also with rods tucked well under her arms, and running behind, hair and cardigan flying in the wind and drizzle, the elderly hostess, with the distracted look of a pursuer. As mystified locals stopped and gawped, and the stray dogs joined in the procession, up the lane they went, left at the junction and on to the small square, then a jerk in the rods took them into a side road and on again. Suddenly, Susy stopped dead in her tracks and looked around. "Here," she said, "this is where they took out the money. They didn't keep the purse, only the money!" Hope sprang. Perhaps there was still a chance of finding the purse. Susy continued to survey the area and then she was on the move again. "There, those bins!" she cried, pointing to three large wheelie bins. "That's where they threw the purse!" They charged across the road to the bins which, to their dismay, had obviously been emptied the previous night. Even though the rods confirmed which bin had in fact held the purse, they had to agree that, even with the help of the faithful rods, no-one was prepared to search through the rubbish on the municipal dump. And so the trail ended there and through no fault of the dowser, or the rods, that particular quest had failed. Jen bought a new purse and the hostess changed her locks.

Often the search for lost items and treasure proves fruitless for a variety of reasons. Sometimes they have already been found and removed, other times the point of loss is not sufficiently accurate. However, occasionally the search will provide an unexpected tale. Such was the case when Jacki's visiting sister lost a ring. Believing that it had been dropped in the garden and knowing that her sister was proficient with the rods, she suggested Jacki dowse for it. Standing near the position her sister indicated, Jacki asked the rods to show her lost treasure and the rods swung vigorously to a huge and ancient carob tree. Believing there must be some mistake Jacki repeated her request and again the rods moved strongly and unerringly to exactly the same position. Knowing, without doubt, that it was not her sister's ring that was drawing the rods, she was anxious to discover more. She moved closer to the tree, which although appearing like one tree with a forked root, was in fact two trees growing side by side in a 'V' shape as they each strove for light. Testing her rods with more questions, she became convinced that she had stumbled on hidden treasure, possibly, she thought, hidden to preserve it during the 'Troubles'. Feeling now that she needed support and confirmation, she called on Bob. Together they retraced her steps and confirmed all she had already found.

The trees themselves proved to be significant. Although huge they turned out to be not that old. The north-facing and larger tree proved to be 180 years old, while the south-facing tree, a sapling from the original, was five years younger. The rods indicated that the treasure was indeed there and had been buried between the roots 88 years ago in 1930. Realising that their original assumption over the reason for the burial was wrong, they re-directed their questioning.

The 'treasure' consisted of around 60 coins mainly silver. (These were a mixture of both Turkish and Greek and must have been antique coins as the coinage of the day was British-based and bronze.) The coins, along with some Greek and Turkish gold jewellery, were enclosed in a metal box 12 inches long and buried 5 feet underground.

The troubling questions remained 'Why was this treasure buried and who had buried it?'

Again, the rods were ready to disclose a story in fascinating detail. A 61-year-old English man, married to a 53-year-old Turkish woman, both obviously now long dead, were visiting relatives in Ozankoy from their home in Nicosia. While in the village they took the opportunity to pilfer from neighbours of their family members. Presumably, anxious to escape detection, they decided to bury the swag and retrieve it later. They chose the most distinctive spot in the area on an unoccupied field. The large carob would be easily recognised on a future occasion.

Sadly, for us, their story ends there. The thieving couple obviously never had an opportunity to return and collect the booty and the dowsers were left with an intense desire to scrape out all the stones and soil that had filled the roots between the trees and dig down for the box, but this was not to be. The area under the trees had been built up, filled in, levelled and netted to make a beautifully shady and protected home for a family of tortoises and they certainly must not be disturbed to assuage curiosity and for a few silver coins!

The lemon on the right is a normal large lemon. The one on the left has been grown over a negative energy line.

Susy was amazed to see her photograph, taken immediately after she has moved an energy line, outside the Vatican

The wizard looks on (back left) as a group of interested, Islamic tourists join in the dowsing at the famous archaeological site in eastern Turkey, Gobeklitepe, which has reputedly re-written history

Right: A group of dowsers inspect the 'blood-letting' tanks at Akdeniz.

Below: A drone hovers over Salamis. Dowsers found a grid of energy lines, passing between the columns. The stones, centre of picture, mark a powerful portal.

Energy orbs surround Susy and fellow dowsers in the cave at Kaleburnu.

The larger, male figure lies with his head to the north.

The female, very negative figure has her head to the south.

Aphendrika

Left: Panaghia Chrysiotissa Church (Church 2)

Right: Panaghia Asomatos Church (Church 3)

An artist's impression of the Aphendrika village square between the churches in early mediaeval times. It has been suggested that the 15ft high walkways were possibly atop walls which protected the square.

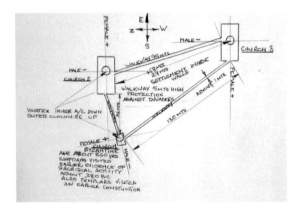

The carved head above the cave-room entrance at Kumyali.

The steps leading down to the three cave-rooms at Kumyali — normal human size to the left, and giant, alien steps to the right.

The marked portal in Maria's garden.

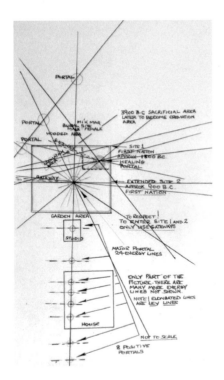

The diagram shows the energy lines that run through Maria's extraordinary property, and the portals that are associated with them. It is not to scale and has been exploded for clarity.

Is this the spirit of a lost loved one, guiding and guarding the singers?

This is believed to be the energy from a portal.

The two women to the right of these pictures, in direct line with an orb, believed that they had been visited by a spirit.

A rune-stone nestles in the sheltered waters of Mahone Bay, Nova Scotia.

The detailed carving shows
the Viking legend.

Chapter Ten

– ENTRY TO THE –
WORLD OF SPIRITS

The moonlight streamed through the landing window casting eerie shadows on the marble floors below. The air was warm and very still, the silence palpable. There was no indication of what had woken her from her deep and happy sleep as she tiptoed to the doorway and listened. Not a sound disturbed the total peace. The air seemed to vibrate and yet she wasn't scared. Then suddenly, as she watched, the shadows took shape and a young girl, so like herself, drifted seamlessly across the space and through the moonbeams, passing silently into another world, a world beyond.

◆━•━○━•━▶

Their visit to Brenda's had made both our witch and wizard more conscious of the unsettled spirits from the 'other world' which, apparently, roam freely among us.

For the scribe, as well for many readers, however, this produced a considerable intellectual challenge. Accustomed, as a scientist, to being able to test theories and provide tangible evidence, this level of dowsing was quite beyond her experience and comprehension. When dowsing for water or lost items, the results were obvious, even if the means were not understood, and she was satisfied by the explanations given of detection of minute changes in electromagnetic fields. However, this was an entirely new and obscure sphere.

Hours of research merely resulted in numerous anecdotes of ghostly sightings or strange and unexplained happenings. Stories of psychic contact with the dead and messages from spirits via a medium or a Ouija board are commonplace and have extended back into folklore, but this did not provide adequate evidence to explain what Bob and Susy were finding.

Then, during the course of writing she came across Sir Roger Penrose's research into consciousness. Penrose, a highly respected mathematical physicist, scientific philosopher and Fellow of Wadham College, Oxford, has collaborated with numerous renowned scientists including the late Stephen Hawking on research into Quantum Mechanics, Relativity, Space and the Universe. Working with Dr Stuart Hameroff from University of Arizona, he introduced a theory of consciousness based on what they called 'Orchestrated Objective Reduction' (Orch-OR). This states that protein-based microtubules, a structural component of human cells, carry quantum energy information stored at sub-atomic level. While many scientists are still unsure about what exactly consciousness is, the duo believes that it is merely the information stored at a quantum level. But energy cannot be destroyed. A number of well-known scientists, including researchers from the famous Max Planck Institute in Munich, agree that it is this quantum energy that leaves the physical body at death and continues to exist indefinitely. In the words of Dr Hans-Peter Durr, former head of the Max Planck Institute, "The body dies but the spiritual quantum field continues. In this way I am immortal" (ref: Sean Martin, Daily Express 20th August 2018).

If this quantum energy equates with 'consciousness' or 'spirit' or indeed 'soul', it could be the strongest proof we have of an after life. And for the purposes of this book, if the spirit is residual energy then it can be detected by the dowsers' rods.

◆— ○ —○—◆

The scribe was content and ready to continue.

The witch and wizard were not surprised when a tenant newly installed in a property contacted them to say that she was sure the house was haunted. On arriving at the house, they were immediately aware of an antagonistic aura.

The tenant complained of doors banging in the night and terrifying creaking on the stairs, although there was no apparent reason. Dowsing revealed again a violent death. This time it appeared to be that of a young soldier. As the rods reached to make contact with him, his anger and aggression were quite obvious. It was clear that his spirit had to be placated and finally laid to rest, before there could be an improvement in the aura of the property. Susy stretched out her mind to contact him but immediately felt a vigorous resistance. Undeterred, she persevered, calmly reasoning with the spirit.

But, for what seemed like an interminable time, he stubbornly remained immutable. Eventually, Susy sensed a weakening of his resolve, and gradually he faded from the scene. Testing with the rods confirmed that he had finally gone to his rest. In spite of later reports that the night noises had ceased, Susy was left with an overwhelming feeling of unease, a feeling that the whole area was suffused with evil. Considering the location, it put her in mind of the quotation from the mediaeval saint, Hilarion, who is said to have exclaimed, "I looked down on the valley and watched the demons fly".

Shortly afterwards they were summoned to another house where strange things were happening. The owner, a meticulous young man with an eye for detail, became aware that his carefully arranged patio chairs seemed to alter their positions. It was not until he had noticed this on a number of occasions that he realised that, as no-one else had access to his property, this movement was not normal. Knowing that Susy and Bob were not only accomplished dowsers, but also had a keen interest in the paranormal, he invited them to call. It was soon clear that there was no earth energy at work here but a clear case of the hand of a spirit. The source of the mischief was soon identified. The story went back nearly two hundred years and the spirit belonged to an old Greek woman. While she felt no animosity towards the owner of the house but was a true product of her own time and culture, she found it hard to accept that there was no woman in the house and, as the present owner was gay, it was unlikely there would be. There was no malice and she meant no harm but was merely intent on making her presence known. Again, Susy acted as spirit mediator and contacted her directly, explaining in the kindest terms that she was being a 'pain' and achieving nothing but irritation. Susy assured her that her victim loved the house and, even in the absence of a woman, was taking good care of it. And so, reassured that the property was in good hands, the spirit was freed to leave and take her rest. The rods proved she had at last left and no invisible hand moved the seats again.

Very often, when they visited a property, our witch and wizard found that the problem they had been invited to investigate was not the only one in the area. In this case they became aware that the owner's dogs would not go near the steps in the garden that led down to a basement or cellar. If the dogs inadvertently passed near they would become agitated and whine. The rods soon identified that many, many years before there had been a death in the area where the basement then stood and the dogs, like all animals, were ultra-sensitive to the presence of spiritual vibes.

Despite these varied findings our wizard sensed that more had happened on the property. He went for a stroll around the garden and soon picked up very strong signals of a death. Using his rods, he pin pointed a spot of intense mortal negativity. He called for the owner who stood by astounded. Bob had identified the exact location where a previous owner had suffered a fatal heart attack. Before he left the garden, he was guided by the rods to another area, also emanating the negativity of death but this time it was clearly not human. The owner confirmed that again, unerringly, Bob had identified the exact spot where the owner's previous dog had been killed in a fight with a neighbour's dog.

At this point the owner had heard quite enough for one day, and, had he previously harboured any misgivings about the authenticity and veracity of dowsing, he certainly felt he had been provided with enough direct evidence to give him serious food for thought.

On a narrow plateau, overlooking the sea and the Taurus Mountains in the distance, and nestling against the mountains of the Kyrenia range, a lovely property stood in an idyllic setting. Entering, visitors could not fail to be impressed by the warm and positive aura of the house and the generous and relaxed hospitality of the owners.

It was therefore with some surprise that our rod-wielders answered a call to investigate and survey the house and land.

The owners were aware that there had been an early settlement on a site near where the house now stood. Builders, as they excavated to lay the foundations, had found ancient tunnels, aquifers, and a few trinkets in the vicinity. These included small pots and bits of jewellery including a bracelet. The builders, with little understanding of the significance of their findings, had shared this basic information with the owner at the time, but he knew no more. However, the dowsers were not told of this until after they had done their initial investigation.

It took the rods only a short time to confirm that the property adjoined the edge of an ancient Bronze Age site that, like so many others on the island, dated back some 4500 years. The rods completed the story by confirming that the tunnels had been used as a treasury at a time of a conflict that almost certainly caused the demise of the original dwellers.

The dowsers were satisfied that they had been able to confirm for the owner the history of his surroundings, but they guessed that this was merely the start of their task. They felt that the house itself held secrets that would reward their special search.

The owners, delighted to have had their history confirmed, then led the dowsers, without any further comment, into the master bedroom. Here, Susy was immediately aware of a female, spiritual presence near the foot of the bed. Careful questioning of the rods and a considerable degree of psychic intuition revealed a touching story. Three bodies were found to have been buried on the spot where the bedroom now stood. They were three generations of females from one family, grandmother, mother and daughter, who had lived two hundred years ago. As she confirmed the presence of the young child, Susy was seized by a fierce crushing pain across her legs and was for a moment totally paralysed. She realised she was experiencing premonition pains and that they were sending her a message. She was convinced that the child had died in a tragic accident. Her legs were crushed, as she fell under the wheels of a cart. Septicaemia developed, and the child did not survive. The child's mother had died of a wasting disease some years later, while still in her thirties, and was buried alongside her daughter and her mother.

It was the spirit of the young mother that lingered in the house. With the paranoid protectiveness of a mother who had lost her child, she had formed an emotional attachment to the pretty, sensitive and highly intuitive 'lady of the house'. Whenever the husband was away from home, the spirit would lie behind her in bed and protectively wrap her arms around her as a mother would a child. Amid tears of emotion, an awareness of this spirit was admitted. It was obvious that a strong, emotional interdependency had been formed and both were reluctant for that bond to be broken. However, it was inevitable that at some point that connection would have to end, so Susy gently contacted the spirit and having thanked her for her protection, explained that her 'friend' was now independent and even if she left the property she would be supported, safe and loved, and it was now time for the spirit to leave and 'cross over'. The spirit was gently eased from the area and eventually went peacefully to rest.

The rods then indicated the presence of a large cavern deep beneath the corner of the room, with a tunnel passing beneath the walls and continuing out into the grounds. It was now the husband's turn to be surprised by the dowser's skills and his eyes were wide with astonishment as he admitted, that while he knew of the tunnel as there had been considerable subsidence in that area, he never expected it to be detected by the rods.

<hr>

Susy had been asked by a friend if she would 'keep an eye' on his property. It was a lovely, old, village house that had been extensively renovated and was being used as a holiday home. Susy was always conscious that the house had a certain aura, but had never sought to investigate further, believing the atmosphere to be due to the antiquity of the original house. One evening, over a glass of wine, overlooking the mountains, Andrew casually commented that his daughter, when visiting, had asked him about 'the ghost'. Immediately, this alerted Susy's senses and she questioned him closely about what his daughter had seen and any feelings he might have about the property.

His daughter had told him that she had twice seen a young girl drift across the landing at the top of the stairs and disappear into a moon beam. Andrew knew nothing of the history of the house and although he was himself sensitive to emotional and even psychic vibes, he certainly had not been aware of any negativity in his home.

The following day, their interest piqued by the previous day's conversation, the ghost-busters arrived at his door. They quickly picked up a psychic foot-print, but the path was confused. They soon established that there were, in fact, two spirits who were reluctant to leave the house. The young girl, whose spirit had been seen by Andrew's daughter, was identified as the granddaughter of the older woman. Little by little, the history was unravelled. Sensing that, although living in the original house, they were not from the local area, Susy had a strong and violent intuition that they were Armenian. Saying nothing of this to Bob, she left him to use his rods to find the dates that they had occupied the property. The year of their arrival coincided with the time of the expulsion of the Armenians from Anatolia and the rods confirmed that they were members of the Armenian diaspora. Grandmother and granddaughter were devoted to each other and when the granddaughter tragically died of disease at the age of eighteen, the grandmother was distraught. The spirit of the young girl clung to her grandmother and refused to leave her. When the grandmother ultimately died, the two spirits remained together in the home they had both loved.

Andrew was delighted that his daughter's vision had not been an illusion and declared that, as they appeared to be benign spirits and posed no threat to the present occupants of the house, he was happy for them to remain, and he wanted no further action taken.

However, Susy was not sure that they had the whole story and again her highly-tuned intuition proved correct.

A week or so later, Andrew, who was back in England, asked her to call at the house to collect some paperwork for him. He told her, quite specifically, that she would find it inside the heavy, wooden chest in the salon prepared ready in a separate folder.

Eager to learn more of the earlier inhabitants of the house, she invited Bob to accompany her. They moved swiftly through the house to the upper floor, where they were immediately aware of the presence of grandmother. Susy had no problem making contact with the spirit, which seemed to welcome the attention and was willing to telepathically communicate with Susy. When asked why she continued to 'haunt' the house after so many years when her granddaughter seemed to only appear on rare occasions, she replied that she felt that it was her task to 'keep an eye' on the house. She was not entirely happy with the renovations that had been made and was particularly horrified by, as she saw it, the unhygienic practice of placing a bathroom and lavatory next to a bedroom, when she was used to having such facilities well away from the house in a separate 'privy'.

The contact between these two was to provide a number of amusing incidents and was to demonstrate another aspect of telepathic communication. It clearly transcends the barrier of language and is a transfer of concepts and ideas without the encumbrance of specific words. Susy realised that she was to have regular contact with this benign and artful spirit and named her Nane. On this first occasion, when she and

Bob returned to the salon to collect the papers, they found them placed, in their folder, on the top of the chest along with the many ornaments. Expecting to find them inside the chest and convinced that they had not been on the top when they first entered the salon, Susy was sure that Nane had placed them there either to prevent Susy from having to lift the very heavy lid of the chest, or merely to prove her presence.

Understanding that Susy now accepted her, Nane became a regular presence and sometimes caused confusion, irritation and even mild terror. Sometimes, Susy would enter the house to find windows open and curtains floating. Initially she feared that the house had been broken into, but there was never any evidence of this, nothing went missing and the window catches were secure and had to be deliberately opened. Ornaments and effects in the house were moved around and were not found where she had left them. A cleaner refused to return to the house, terrified when she felt a tap on her shoulder from an invisible hand. Susy knew, without doubt, that this was all the work of Nane. After a time, she identified a pattern in the behaviour and realised that Nane's mischief only occurred if she was not greeted by Susy on her arrival.

On another occasion, Susy took a friend Carl with her when she visited the house. She knew that her friend was extremely practical, and she was also aware that he was highly sceptical of her psychic vibes and would not have believed himself sensitive to a spiritual presence. Entering the house, they were both struck by the chill in the air. She went into the downstairs bedroom to turn on the air conditioner unit. The control panel was on the wall and the press button starters were extremely stiff. She had to exert considerable finger pressure to start the unit. She then proceeded to do her normal check of the property. When they were finally ready to leave they returned to the bedroom to turn off the unit. As Carl approached the panel, with his finger poised to press hard on the OFF button, the indicator lights on the panel began to flash and move up and down rapidly. Carl was completely mesmerised and horrified. He could find no rational cause for the flashing lights and the only possible explanation Susy could give was that Nane was, again, up to her tricks and thought she would give him a shock. If this was her aim she most certainly succeeded.

Susy had become familiar with Nane's quirky ways but did ask her to control her antics and not to frighten the family and their friends.

Whether it was due to the presence of Nane or her granddaughter, or to other psychic forces at work, the house seemed to be a sanctuary for spirits. Susy was very aware of this and so she was in no way surprised when Andrew himself experienced an emotionally moving episode.

It had been a couple of years earlier that Andrew had tragically lost a very dear friend to cancer. The loss had been felt keenly. The friend was a highly talented musician and he and Andrew had worked together on projects in the past. Andrew felt he was not only a warm friend but a mentor and guide. He had often felt that when he was composing Mark was with him in spirit encouraging and guiding him. However, at that time he was also working hard on completing a book rather than his usual music. One evening, he was planning to write for a time while waiting for Susy to join him for supper. For some reason he was

conscious of Mark's presence more strongly than usual and so was feeling sensitive and a little emotional. He thought he might find Mark's music calming and so sought through his CDs for a suitable background. Anxious not to over-indulge his emotion he carefully avoided the CD that he knew held Mark's arrangement of "Abide with me" that never failed to reduce him to tears. Assuring himself that he had chosen the suitable CD for his mood he settled back to listen and hopefully to write. Relaxed and warm in the soft embrace of the music he wrote on and was disturbed only by the soft knock when Susy arrived. As he rose to greet her he was conscious of tears streaming down his face as the haunting strains of, the so carefully avoided, "Abide with me" flooded the room.

Chapter Eleven

– BACK FROM THE DEAD –

In a Muslim country where cremation is not allowed, an ageing ex-pat population can put a great strain on land allocated for Christian burial. Some of the older, smaller cemeteries have become overcrowded. Over the years headstones have been lost and the positioning of early bodies was not necessarily recorded.

The working committee of a small cemetery on the outskirts of a mountain village, decided to tidy their overgrown domain and make a record of the bodies buried but not identified. A call was made to 'divine' Bob, who arrived with his rods. He had no difficulty in finding the individual graves. He marked the perimeters and soon a pattern emerged which allowed the committee to record and map the area. But Bob now felt in contact with the spirits of the bodies buried. He was able to determine if the grave had a single occupant or was, in fact, a family grave. He was able to report to the committee secretary whether the occupant of the grave was a man or a woman. He could ascertain the year of death, the age at death and the cause of death. He was building a profile of the occupants of the graves, as clearly as if they were alive and able to speak for themselves. At one point he was observed, working against the wall of the tiny, adjacent church, and clearly distressed. When questioned, he explained that he had stumbled on the grave of a small child.

Susy and Bob were to be called up on several occasions to perform similar surveys. While they readily supplied the valuable practical information that the various committees required, on their own account they accessed some incredible stories from the energy left behind by the bodies that were buried.

When changes are needed to an existing cemetery, there is always concern that graves are not disturbed or in any way desecrated. For this reason, when municipal construction started near to the major Christian cemetery, the boundaries were questioned, and the dowsers were called. One by one they identified the unmarked graves as they made their way around the enclosed area. Bob had identified the resting place of a young man. By carefully phrasing his questions he ascertained that the youth had arrived on the island from Scotland during the 1800s. But when he attempted to locate the depth of the grave he found he was getting very confused results from the rods. He called Susy over to assist. As she approached she experienced a deep sense of disorientation and dread. Combining their efforts, they were able to confirm that deep in the ground beneath this grave was a much older trench, a mass grave, or plague pit, and further investigation indicated that it had been dug at a time when there had been an epidemic on the island which had caused a considerable number of deaths from the disease.

While Bob was concentrating on the history of the epidemic, Susy had wandered off and was busy working near the perimeter. She had found fifteen bodies that were buried outside the existing walls of the cemetery. Among these were two brothers who had been brought from Scotland to be sheep farmers on the island. (This information was confirmed a couple of years later, as a result of research into local records and archives.) Eventually she returned, excited over what she believed was an extraordinary find. She was convinced she had been in contact with the spirit of The Hermit. This man had, for many years, been the subject of much story-telling in the town. Although not a Church member herself, Susy had heard something of the legend of the hermit-priest, who had built the Hermitage and was believed to have been buried in its grounds. She knew no more and was therefore amazed that she had stumbled on his spirit, apparently complaining that he believed that his body, although it had been moved from the Hermitage, lay straddling the boundary of the cemetery and so was not entirely laid in 'hallowed ground'. According to Susy's report of her encounter, he was less than pleased. Later research uncovered more of the story of this interesting and unusual man.

Ambrose Williams was educated at Peterhouse, Cambridge, after which he travelled to South America, where he was subsequently ordained. After flirting briefly with Roman Catholicism, he was reunited with the Anglican Church when he settled for a time in Turkey, and then Cyprus. He built the Hermitage as his home in 1945 and became a recluse. Detaching himself from both his fellow men and the Church, he lived the life of a monk or hermit. He never visited the local Anglican Church of St Andrew's, though it was known that Archdeacon Goldie visited him regularly to hear his confession. (One can only wonder at the sins he felt he must confess!) He died in 1957, bequeathing the Hermitage to the Jerusalem and East Mission to be held in trust "for the benefit and use of the Anglican Church in Cyprus". While at the time of his death he was buried in the grounds, in 1965, fearing that the building may be sold, church members relocated his body to the local cemetery. It was here, over 50 years later, that Susy had found his grave, identified him, and then made psychic contact with his spirit, which still lingered at the spot (ref: 'A short story of St Andrews English Church, Kyrenia, Cyprus' by P.C. Collins, BD).

Once again history had confirmed the message from the rods.

Just as Bob had found the body of a baby discreetly buried near the wall of the smaller cemetery he had visited, so here, Susy was observed visibly upset near the wall in a far corner of the grounds. Again, it was the body of a baby that had been buried unofficially and one is left to imagine the distress and trauma that had led to such a situation.

Susy was then called to a cool, pleasant spot shaded by a large, spreading carob tree. Beneath the tree she found the body of a young woman, whose spirit had not passed over. She had died in child birth and appeared desperate for someone to acknowledge that her child had been a little girl. Susy made psychic contact with the spirit and although there was still an aura of strong emotion, it appeared that just imparting her story to Susy had given the mother peace and her spirit found its rest.

While Susy and Bob are both supremely confident in the accuracy of the results they achieve, and these, in practical cases like position and depth of water and location of pipes and even graves, can be readily verified and cannot be challenged, other areas of their work are not as easy to defend. Many people are highly sceptical when they are provided with information such as details of the occupants of graves. It is therefore very satisfying for them to have their findings confirmed by an independent source, as in the case of the two Scottish brothers and Father Ambrose.

Another example of this was after a visit to grounds near the church where excavation work for construction was about to start.

Many stories were still told among the locals about fighting that had been seen in that area during the troubled years. There was some concern that there may have been bodies buried there, left from that time, and therefore some anxiety that, if that was the case, they may be desecrated by the building. And so, our body-finders were contacted.

The night before their appointment on the site, our witch had a violent dream that proved to be a premonition. There was a strong portent of death and she woke sweating and shaking from the experience. She was in no doubt that this unexpected and unusual experience was related to their intended visit. And so, it was with some trepidation that she approached the area. Before long the dowsers had discovered the basis of her dream. Bob revealed that there had been fighting at the spot where they were dowsing and that two young men had died, one Turkish Cypriot and one

Greek Cypriot. The municipal workmen moved carefully with their JCBs, but they found no bodies. However, they did uncover the remains of an old pillbox and some sand bags, both of which provided evidence that there had been a serious battle in that location. It was in the pillbox that the Turkish Cypriot died as he tried to defend the area.

Bob dowsed again and confirmed that while he had identified the spot where they each died, the bodies had been removed at the time. Even though the bodies were no longer on the site, their original presence had left a strong psychic impression on the area. Bob decided to follow the trail. Unfortunately, traces of the Greek Cypriot youth were soon lost, and it was believed that his body was collected by friends or family and taken away in a vehicle for a Christian burial. The trail of the Turkish Cypriot proved easier and Bob was able to follow it along the coast to the east until it was finally committed to the sea some half mile or so out of town.

Satisfied that no bodies were on the site the municipal builders were able to continue with easy minds.

It was a couple of months later when one of the Church wardens, who had been present at the dowsing, sought out Bob at a party. He excitedly told Bob that, having been fascinated by the findings on the day, he had spent numerous hours since, scouring the archives and had finally found written records of the two men who had died on that fateful day in 1971.

It was as a result of these encounters with the dead, that they realised that their abilities could add much to the normal historical records of archaeological sites. Through their skill at contacting the spirits of those who had died in an area, they could discover much about the lives of the fallen and could therefore put a more human face to history.

This formed a major interest in a visit to Salamis.

The history and archaeology of the ancient Greek city-state of Salamis on the south-eastern coast of Northern Cyprus has been extensively documented. Although there has been little excavation since the troubled period of the 1960s and 70s the area is well preserved, publicised and visited. During the latter part of the 19th and the first half of the 20th century considerable archaeological work was carried out and numerous artefacts are displayed in the British Museum in London. While it is recorded that the Greeks, visiting the island to trade for copper in the late Bronze Age, established their city-state in the 11th century BC, it is believed by some to be built over a much older settlement. The Greeks were ultimately superseded by the Assyrians in the 9th century BC and the island was ruled by them. The history of the area is rich.

But this, and much more, can be found in historical and archaeological reports and even Wikipedia. To probe the history further was, therefore, not the main intention of our witch and wizard when they took a group of enthusiastic dowsers to the site for a day. On this occasion they were keen to investigate the planning of the major buildings on the site and study any related energy fields.

Their starting point was the gymnasium, which, with its many columns bravely demarking the boundary and still impressive, must have been a magnificent sight in its day. As expected the appearance of the dowsing rods brought a small group of inquisitive tourists to observe the proceedings. Many remained fascinated as the rods reported the findings.

It came as no surprise, particularly to the more experienced members of the group, that the site was criss-crossed by energy lines. However, the positioning of the columns in relation to the energy lines left no doubt that the original Greek builders had been familiar with the power and significance of earth energy lines and had the ability to detect them. The lines actually ran in straight lines across the area, approximately east to west, linking the columns on opposite sides of the field. Other lines linked the pillars on the north and south borders. At the crossing point of a number of these energy lines there was a stone structure, which obviously marked the position of the portal which the dowsers detected. As the energy entering this portal was strong and about a metre wide, the witch and wizard decided to use this to demonstrate their ability to cut, or hold back an energy line. Making sure that every member of the group had confirmed the position of the energy they placed them all behind an imaginary line stretching across the energy line and about three metres from the portal. Then, starting at diagonal corners of the rectangle they had produced, they strode purposefully and slowly around the area, striking the ground regularly with their long poles. When they had each completed the full circuit they invited the group members to check within the area for evidence of the original energy line. There was none. However, particularly sensitive dowsers reported that they had been very aware of a build-up of energy where they were standing, particularly a tingling in the feet and legs, presumably caused by the 'back-up' of energy as the flow was stopped in its tracks.

Anxious not to disturb the natural flow of earth energy, the two then proceeded to reverse their actions and the amazed dowsers confirmed that the energy line had been restored.

Susy then went on to discover the death of a young guard not far from the portal. He had been in his twenties and had been fighting with another guard over the disputed courtship of a pretty girl.

Bob then went on to confirm that the Greeks had been followed by the Romans, and his rods found the evidence that a young Roman soldier had been cut down by a sword and had lain near the edge of the gymnasium near to the communal latrines.

Certainly, the tourists, Turkish as well as Germans and Swiss, who had watched and listened enthralled, and even at times excitedly asked questions, would have had an unusual tale to tell when they returned to their hotels.

The group moved on from the gymnasium to the well-preserved amphitheatre. Many of the dowsers were very familiar with the incredible acoustic properties of an ancient amphitheatre. Some had previously stood, centre stage, at this very spot, or in the amphitheatre of Kyrenia, or Delphi, and whispered messages, audible at the highest point of the terraces. Although thespian skills were again inevitably tested, on this occasion, it was earth energy rather than sound transmission that was focus of attention. The dowsers spread out around the theatre tracking various earth energy lines and before long it became obvious that energy lines radiated outwards from a focal point at the centre of the lower floor reaching the outer ring of the amphitheatre and inevitably the focus coincided with the focal point of sound. Although each member of the group independently confirmed this, so far there has been no scientific explanation of the synchronicity.

Again, the dowsers returned home with considerable scope for further investigation, having experienced a very different view of this ancient site than their previous purely archaeological or touristic visits.

Chapter Twelve

– DOWSING FOR HEALTH –

Our very practical wizard had no previous experience in the esoteric arts associated with faith, psychic or pranic healing, but harboured very strong feelings about the value of fresh and uncontaminated food and a strong aversion to the modern-day practice of looking for a pharmaceutical answer to every slight mental or physical malady.

Both he and Susy were most anxious to use their skills to help people discover for themselves the possible cause of their medical disorders and find a more natural remedy.

They do not pretend to be doctors. They never prescribe and will only advise. They both believe in the importance of balance in the body and are both convinced that many symptoms are the direct result of physical or emotional disturbance or imbalance. They believe the effect on the body of the negative energy or black-water that they have observed is a clear example of this disturbance. In many cases, these symptoms, once recognised, can be relieved by the restoration of body equilibrium by a simple change in diet or life-style.

For Bob these irregularities and their causes are revealed through the rods, whereas, although Susy can use rods, pendulum or just her hands, there are occasions when Susy only needs to approach a person and their mental or physical problems are revealed to her directly through her 'third eye'.

After years of experience now, Bob also receives an instinctive response to serious health problems even when there are no outward signs of the condition. This happens particularly with undiagnosed cancer and conditions like diabetes.

In the early days of their divining for health, neither had any idea how these messages came to them. However, in more recent years there has been intense medical research on the different wave lengths of energy emitted by healthy and diseased organs. These wave lengths can be detected by specifically designed meters which will display them as colours. Comparisons between the colours emitted by healthy organs and diseased ones show a marked difference (ref. Dr Harry Oldfield – Kirlian photography 'The dark side of the brain').

Sadly, these techniques have not been adopted by the mainstream medical profession. Similarly, there is increasing medical evidence that dogs can detect abnormal medical conditions such as diabetes or cancer. The belief is that they are hypersensitive to changes in the chemical balance and can, for example, distinguish by smell, an increase in blood or urine, sugar or protein levels and perhaps unusual chemicals produced by an offensive tumour.

Such findings have led our dowsers to consider that this may be a clue to their own ability to detect problems. Is their own general hypersensitivity to minute changes in electromagnetic fields and slight chemical alterations the key to their own diagnostic abilities?

For Bob, this started some years ago when a visiting friend asked him if the rods could determine the cause of the pain in her leg. He realised, although sceptical of success, it was worth a try. She lay on the carpet and he scanned her with the rods. He immediately identified which leg had the problem although it had not affected her gait and so there was no outward indication. It was clear that the rods were not satisfied, and he went on to confirm that the true problem stemmed from the back. This amazed the friend as she had made no connection between her leg pain and an old back injury. She was then able to work on back-strengthening exercises and the pain in the leg was eventually gone.

Before long he had friends clamouring for his rods' diagnoses. One had a rash and wasn't sure whether it was an infection or an allergy. The rods readily dismissed any possibility of an infection and, unfortunately for the sufferer, identified an allergy to strawberries, so abundant on the island and so sweet. With great sadness, the fruits were removed from the diet and immediately the rash disappeared.

At certain social occasions, queues would form as folks waited patiently to have their allergies checked. Even those who had been diagnosed by a doctor seemed anxious to have their sensitivities confirmed. All expressed surprise, particularly those that admitted they had already known about their condition and had not expected to have it so readily identified. A surprising number of people appear to be allergic to gluten and also to dairy products. These allergies have been recognised for many years, but it is less well acknowledged that in numerous cases it is not the food itself that is responsible for the allergy but additives, particularly colourants, artificial flavourings and preservative agents. This is especially true when the allergy is shown to be to wine. This diagnosis can be stressful to wine-lovers, but it need not be a terminal disaster. The rods can be clinically specific. As well as clearly differentiating between red and white wine they can also indicate certain additives in the wine. The most common case is when the wine has been produced from grapes that have been subjected to intense insecticides and it is that, rather than the alcohol, that is producing the allergic reaction. A change to a wine from an insecticide-free region may allow the former sufferer to enjoy his or her drink in the future, symptom-free.

Both Susy and Bob find it infinitely rewarding when people return, sometimes months later, to thank them for their advice, confirming that the symptoms, whether itchy rash, nausea or pain, seem to have gone for good.

The diagnostic skills of the rods are not confined to detecting allergic reactions as has already been suggested. By using a similar counting method to that used to find the depth of water, blood pressure can be measured. By defining a scale of 1–5 or 1–10, blood sugar or cholesterol levels can be measured against an acceptable mean. If these results are checked by conventional meters like a blood-pressure cuff, the rods, in the hands of a skilled dowser, are amazingly accurate.

However, dowsing for health problems brings an enormous responsibility to the dowsers. As both Susy's and Bob's sensitivity increased they became ever more aware of the general physical condition of the people that presented themselves. It has already been said that Susy does not need to use either rods or pendulum to know instinctively if someone is experiencing a totally invisible problem. A hand resting in a particular part of the body or often directly on a chakra will tell her clearly the nature of the problem. Sometimes she is able to give instant reassurance, other times a suggested quick remedy. But, inevitably, for both our witch and wizard, there will be the odd occasion when neither of these is appropriate. There are times when their own protocols demand that they deny their skills and will not share with the sufferer their findings. They may allay unnecessary fear with a reassuring smile and the querulous words, "I don't know! Maybe you should have a blood test or see your doctor".

The burden of silence is great and the entire process of any form of health determination is emotionally exhausting.

Very recently Bob had the opportunity to use a newly acquired skill of 'Remote Viewing', to support a practitioner in another country. A young friend from Germany, we'll call her Beata, had qualified in alternative medical procedures and she had opened a clinic providing treatment to cancer patients. The course had its basis in the boosting of the patient's immune system to enable it to fight the cancer from within. This meant that she would only accept patients who were in the early stages of the disease and who had not undergone chemotherapy which annihilates the immune system. However, she was approached by the distraught mother of a young girl who had a large and malignant tumour on her neck. She had received one course of chemotherapy and had not reacted well. Her oncologist had given them very little hope if she did not undergo further chemotherapy. The child knew the possible consequences of refusing further conventional treatment but was adamant that she did not wish to proceed with the chemo. Her mother had respected her child's wishes and had acquiesced. Although aware of the much lower chance of success, she was delighted to be accepted for the alternative treatment and was optimistic.

At first, Beata had been concerned over the child's weakened immune system but much moved by the tragic situation and heartened by the child's spirit she had agreed to accept her for treatment. Initially, there seemed no progress and the tumour appeared to be still growing. She contacted Bob and asked if he could 'view' the condition from a distance and advise her. He had never tried to do this before and had little hope of success, but he asked Beata to send him digital photos of the child showing the tumour.

He opened up the pictures on his computer screen and using the rods over the screen he concentrated hard on the tumour and asked his questions. He asked the same questions several times over the next couple of days, and consistently received the same answers. This was the information that he gained from the rods, which he passed on to Beata.

The tumour would continue to grow steadily for the next 10 days, but would then rupture and suppurate for a couple of days. It would then close over and appear to heal but would gradually swell again over the next few weeks. However, it would eventually rupture as before and this time would heal and no longer grow.

Beata was delighted with the prediction. She had great faith in Bob's ability with the rods and drew great confidence from his message. She spoke with the child and her mother who, at long last, felt they had some hope.

The latest news from Germany was that the path of the tumour had followed the exact course that Bob had predicted. The final rupture took place about 6 months ago and the happy, healthy and bright child is back in full-time school, achieving well.

It is possibly unnecessary to note that child, mother and practitioner, all drew strength from the prediction and, while amazed at its accuracy, could not have been more grateful and delighted. He had not cured, or in fact taken part in the physical healing process, but perhaps the hope Bob's prediction had given had played some psychological part in the successful healing process. He would certainly hope so.

Just as this volume was to be sent to the publisher, another interesting case appeared. Bob received an email from Canada. It was from his son, Steven, whom you will meet again later.

Steven's neighbour needed Bob's help. The young wife had been receiving treatment for breast cancer and her husband was looking for any means of alternative medicine that could give her support. They also had a thirteen-year-old daughter, who was very bright but had serious sleep problems and severe concentration difficulties. The neighbour discussed the situation with Steven, unaware that Steven and his father were involved with dowsing. He was familiar with water-dowsing as he had watched his own father dowsing for a well on their farm, when he was a child. Steven told him a little about Bob's activities but did not suggest he attempt to assist. However, he immediately contacted Bob.

Armed with the full address of the neighbour, Bob sought the property on Google Earth. He was able to obtain a very clear view of all aspects of the property and was, of course, familiar with the general area, although it was four thousand miles from where he was sitting. As soon as the picture came up on the screen he was conscious of the usual churning in his stomach indicating negative energy. Taking up his rods he searched the property and found a broad, very strong black-water and negative earth energy line running parallel down one side of the house passing through the living room on the ground floor, and through the bathroom and child's bedroom on the first floor.

Bob then suggested to Steven that he should take his rods to his friend's house and check the findings. A very excited Steven Skyped that evening to inform his father that he had confirmed the exact position of the black-water and that it ran into the well. He said that the family had a very sophisticated water filter but had already decided that in spite of chemical tests on the water, it was, for some inexplicable reason, unfit to drink. Bob had assessed that the width of the black-water was about a metre and Steven confirmed that it was between one and two metres wide. Steven also noted that along the line of the negative energy the trees were stunted and dying, and the fruit on them was gnarled and distorted.

Further discussion with the neighbour confirmed that the child had suffered the same symptoms as long as they had lived in the house, but had been completely free of the problem, sleeping well and always 'top-of-the-class' during the time they had lived in Argentina.

The following morning, Bob set to work in earnest. He again called up the property on Google Earth. Surveying the immediate area he saw that a new house was being built directly opposite and the malignant black-water was running straight through it. Fortunately, behind the house was uninhabited woodland so Bob saw his opportunity. Summoning all his psychic power, he gradually eased the negative energy away from the house and directed it in a channel between the adjoining houses and safely out to the woodland. He tracked the black-water for more than two hundred metres from the house, in a forested area, and turned it into the ground. He then checked with the rods and confirmed that the negativity had left the property

It may be some weeks before the family feels the beneficial effects of this action. The child's sleep patterns have been disturbed for some time and it may take time to establish normal sleep. However, there is an expectation that her levels of concentration may improve very rapidly and that she will again be at the top-of-the-class.

Chapter Thirteen

– STEP BACK INTO HISTORY –

Responding to the demand for more experiences, our witch and wizard gathered around them a group of eager acolytes and arranged a trip along the north coast of Cyprus to the site of the cave city of Lambousa and the ancient fish ponds. As the dowsers scrambled along the uneven path towards the shore, the square structures of the 'ponds' were clearly visible beneath the waters of even the high tide. Careful observation showed that while fresh cold sea water flowed over at high tide the warmer stagnant water at low tide washed through side channels thus ensuring that fish stored in the ponds were kept fresh.

The rods gave no indication that the area was, in fact, the 'legendary' Atlantis as had been suggested, but there was considerable confirmation and expansion of the long-standing history of the area. Historians have recorded the use of the fish ponds from as early as 3000BC when they were the earliest of their kind. This was the late Neolithic period and the native people would still have been living in caves or primitive huts.

The bay was eventually to be an ancient Roman port and the ponds were used to protect freshly caught fish. While confirming this with the rods one of the more sensitive dowsers reported that her rods had identified the far easterly pond, which was raised higher from the tide-line, as being used for fresh water and stocked with piranha. As she failed to question the rods further, one can only guess what they were used for, but a certain James Bond film comes to mind!

Turning their attention inland to the rock city of Lambousa, the group were tacitly and warily greeted by the ancient, bearded shepherd, self-appointed, intermittent guardian of the site. This devotee, with the chiselled features and piercing, but sensitive, eyes of a true Ottoman, watched the group's activities with interest, at first from a distance, then carefully moving closer, becoming part of the proceedings. Finally convinced that no harm was intended, he confided, in mono-verbal English and much gesturing, that the caves had been a monastery. He mimed that a baby had been buried in a far corner and that on the land above the 10 metre cliff was the burial site for the settlement. Having watched for a time, imparted his vital information, and still wearing a slightly bewildered look, he eventually drifted away to find his flock.

The Lambousa area has a long and varied history with records back 5000 years. However, the rods indicated the existence of much earlier dwellers, as far back as 8000BC, which would suggest some of the earliest Neolithic settlers but sadly unlike in Paphos, here, they had left no archaeological traces.

The rods of the individual dowsers added a wealth of details to the background. While it is generally acknowledged that the caves had various uses over the years, including comprising part of a monastery, dwelling places for fishermen, store houses and tombs, the area had a much longer and richer story.

The island of Cyprus was readily accessible by even primitive sea-faring folk and so its shores saw many visitors. Some were merely curious, others came to trade while still others recognised the tell-tale pale green streaks of copper carbonate in the sandy-coloured soil and so, during the Bronze Age, the abundance of copper ore fed men's greed and they arrived to conquer.

The rods identified the Syrians arriving in about 5800BC, but history does not record this arrival, possibly for two reasons: Syria, at the time, was not a distinct country but was an area of Phoenicia and yet the rods differentiated it; secondly, these early visitors were almost certainly driven out by the warring Hittites or even an ancient indigenous race. These aggressive Hittites were to play an important role in the history of both Cyprus and the Turkish mainland. They were originally Steppe-herders from north-east of the Black Sea who gradually moved west and settled for a time in the area that is now central Europe. Eventually they migrated south, settling in Anatolia, a large region of central Turkey. Groups of these ancestral Turkish may have travelled across from the mainland as early 5000BC, although conventional history gives this time as two millennia later, at the time of the first Bronze Age. This was the period of the Old Testament stories when the Canaanites roamed the Levant, although it is difficult to calculate, as early chroniclers dated events from the assumed creation, anno mundi. By the year 2000BC civilisation, such as it was, had moved into the second Bronze Age and Man still had a need for copper. This brought the Egyptians, the Mycenaeans and the Phoenicians. The Egyptians never colonised but they did leave an impression strong enough to be detected by the dowsing rods. The Phoenicians, who included people from the areas that we now know as Syria, Lebanon and Israel, were most certainly colonisers. They were followed half a millennium later by the Greeks and then Romans. All arrivals were faithfully reported by the rods.

Archaeological finds towards the end of the 19th century and into the early 20th century and early writings, that have been unearthed, have shown that Lambousa was founded as a colony after the Trojan War in about 1000BC.

In the 4th century BC it was described as one of the nine Cypriot City Kingdoms.

The rods confirmed the overlay of uses of the caves throughout that history. They located the exact position of the buried baby reported by the shepherd-guardian. They also found the resting place of a 62-year-old priest. The bodies of three Roman soldiers, dating from 100BC, were discovered in the burial ground above the rock city. A dowser went on to investigate the causes of their death and the message he received through the rods was so strong that he was visibly overcome with tears of emotion and had to leave the site, in order to restore his calm. One of the soldiers was only 24 years of age when he died by garrotting, the second was 29 and was killed with a blow from an axe, while the third was 33 and died of septicaemia rather than by a violent death. All the messages from the area were strong and were corroborated by each of the dowsers.

The archaeological digs of the last hundred years have revealed treasures that suggest that the Romans built a magnificent walled city on the site. There are remains of the Roman fortress walls. It is believed that in the early years of Christianity, Lambousa was visited not only by Cyprus-born St Barnabas, but was passed through by St Mark, and also Paul of Tarsus, who we know was renowned for his travels to Malta and Rome.

Silver vases, pots and spoons with animal motifs on their rims have been unearthed, each marked with the Byzantium Imperial stamp, suggesting that they were brought to the affluent city from the Byzantine capital, Constantinople. In 1902, two plates commemorating David and Goliath were discovered and the stamp on them dates them between 627 and 630 AD. A wealth of treasure was found at this time but sadly only a small number of items remained on the island and are exhibited in the Museum in south Nicosia. Most artefacts were removed and can now be viewed in museums in Washington, New York, London and Paris.

"The Lambousa treasure is a reflection of the high standard of early Byzantine art during the 6th and 7th centuries and is indicative of Lambousa's wealth and level of social development at the time." (Wikipedia).

There is some suggestion by Byzantine historians that the fish ponds were, in fact, bathing pools attached to a wealthy villa. However, the rods gave not the slightest evidence of this.

The fabulous city was drastically damaged by an Arab invasion in the late 7th century AD and it is highly likely that the treasures had been buried deliberately at the time, in order to preserve them.

Further questioning of the rods suggested that the Templars had at least visited the area around 1200AD which would fit in with their presence on the island during the 3rd and disastrous 4th Crusades.

The dowsing group, while exhausted, felt they had experienced an amazing insight into the past and could not wait for their next trip.

The headland of Sardunya shows the rods evidence of similar settlements as in other coastal areas, with expected habitation of various races over periods of time. Some of these tribes were wiped out by battles but there was also strong evidence of devastation caused by two separate earthquakes and subsequent tsunamis. Those who, mercifully, have never experienced the force of earthquake, volcano or tsunami, can have little idea of the destructive force they generate and the vast distances over which they can exert an effect.

Some 30 miles east of Sardunya on a relatively lonely stretch of Alagadi Beach archaeologists and geologists are still picking up small particles of white pumice, clearly visible among the grains of sand and rocks. This volcanic deposit, they have proved, was spewed from the earth's core during the eruption on the Greek island of Santorini. This massive event took place in 1540BC towards the end of the second Bronze Age and yet, even after three and a half thousand years, the evidence is still there on the beach, carried by the tidal currents nearly 500 miles.

Travelling west along the north coast of the island, one will eventually reach the idyllic village of Akdeniz or Ayia Irini, Sacred Peace in Greek. Nestling on a fertile plain on the very eastern fringe of Morphou Bay, this rural farming community, could, at first glance, be still living centuries back in time.

The area is well known to archaeologists as, in 1920, the Swedish/Cypriot Archaeological expedition obtained permission from the British colonists to excavate. Ayia Irini, like Lambousa, was one of the early City Kingdoms and had been inhabited for an extended period by the Phoenicians. It was mainly their artefacts, left behind towards the end of the second Bronze Age and the end of the Archaic Period, that provided the 1927–31 dig with their richest finds. No less than 3000 items were recovered, some of them in amazingly pristine condition. Other pieces from a revival period during the first century BC were also found.

While, sadly, it was part of the original agreement that half the treasures should leave the island and be exhibited in the Museum of Mediterranean Antiquities in Stockholm, the other half remained and can be seen in various museums on the island. However, in a remarkable joint historical and artistic project, the whole collection has been brought to life, as copies of many of the artefacts recovered have been reproduced in terracotta and are now on display for all to see. Statuettes, figurines, headgear and fashion, jewellery, votive offerings, war chariots, animals and minotaurs, all take their place alongside other effects from the time, to provide a fascinating insight into ancient people and their lives.

The tombs from which many of these treasures were taken are now protected, but Akdeniz still holds many secrets not yet fully explored.

While the rods confirm many of the findings as Roman in accordance with the official dating, they also indicate that the site was used much earlier for dwellings which had been occupied over millennia by no less than eleven different races including the Hittites. Most of the earliest living quarters are still buried at least 5 metres beneath the present surface.

A climb to a vantage point, not far from the tombs, will reveal large square and oblong carved indentations in the natural rocks. At first, they could be mistaken for footbaths. On closer inspection, however, channels will be discovered entering and leaving the rock tanks and the rods readily disclose the sinister use of these structures. They date back to the earlier Neolithic period and were part of a dark sacrificial ceremony. The dowsers were to encounter these tanks on many of the sites they visited on the island. The channels were for the letting of blood in human sacrifice. On this site in Akdeniz there were three tanks. These appeared to be for separate sacrifices; one for young females, another for young males, all between eight and twelve years of age, and a third one for new-born babies. The ceremonies for the new-borns would take place twice a year at the winter and summer Solstice but that for pre-pubescent children took place six times a year. It was believed that such sacrifices would increase fertility, both of their crops and their race, and that drinking the blood would increase life expectancy. There was also an area that had clearly been used for animal sacrifice during the same period. The rods also indicated that there were special entrances to each sacrificial site.

Moving away from this grim and negative scene towards a deep rift which in the past had been a rich river valley, the rods indicated the burial place of large numbers of dwarf hippo bones, another sign of the changes in natural life on the island over the centuries. In earlier times the presence of dwarf species would have been typical of island fauna due to the limitation of food supplies.

On the rim of the rift there are steps leading down to a rock cave. Strangely there are two sets of steps, one with normal width treads and drop, and the other giant steps. At the base of the steps is a rocky platform. Here the dowsing rods became very active. The area was highly energetic with ley lines passing through in several directions. It was clear the centre of this plateau was a portal and had served an important purpose in earlier times. The rods indicated that the steps had continued down to the valley floor which indeed had held a wide river estuary in the past with direct access to the nearby sea. The site had undoubtedly been a port and possibly the cave higher up had been used for storage.

The more experienced dowsers were not satisfied that they had found all the answers to the area and continued to question the rods about the strange steps. They were to discover a similar situation in another site and all was then revealed.

Conscious that the whole area had been an important settlement in very early times and so carried some of the residual energy of these earlier inhabitants, our wizard was not surprised when he was approached by a friend who lived in the village. She would not have described herself as a dowser nor was she aware that she was particularly sensitive to earth or spiritual energy. However, she was in the habit of walking her dog across fields, on the south of the village and well inland from the area known to our dowsers. She would take a rest on a large, flat stone near a small copse of shady trees. It was here that she became conscious of feelings that she experienced nowhere else and felt strongly that there was a spiritual presence.

It was immediately clear that this was an area worthy of the scrutiny of a team of dowsers and so it became the site of the next expedition.

With little guidance the wizard pinpointed the spot and the witch set to work to organise teams to investigate. Each team was given an area and a recorder was appointed for each group. They were then given a list of questions to ask the rods.

Before long the history of the area began to take shape. It had been a Neolithic settlement dating back 8 to 9000 years. Two distinct time periods were in evidence, the second being some 2000 years later. Soon tape measures and markers appeared and the position of dwellings were identified and the exact location and dimensions of the two temples. There were the, now, very familiar altars for sacrifice, some clearly for humans and others for animals. Again, there was a special place for the sacrifice of pre-pubescent girls. The characteristic stone tanks were also present showing the grooves for the blood-letting.

One experienced dowser reported that she had passed over hidden caverns or caves which were very possibly underground dwellings dating back to the Stone Age, troglodytes, but time did not allow a more extensive investigation.

There was some indication of land slippage either caused by erosion or earth tremors. The area was vast and like so many of the other places visited certainly would reward further study.

Travelling east towards the panhandle, the Karpaz peninsula, there are numerous outcrops of Neolithic remains.

Some of these are semi-exposed tombs which have been dug out and plundered over the ages. There are the remnants of ancient wells and even sacrificial sites that undoubtedly hold close many secrets of the past, but there are not the resources to officially exploit them.

A keen and observant walker, exploring a remote way-marked track beyond the village of Sipahi, might just spy, among the heavy ground-cover, two large lumps of dark rock. On closer inspection he will see that they are, in fact, huge, roughly worked figures.

For a sensitive dowser, however, the area is immediately repelling, with a similar head-clamping, gut-wrenching aura of negativity that many experienced to the west of the Baspinar plateau.

The inquisitive rambler would observe that the figures are lying at different angles and that both had, at some point, been pushed off their supporting plinths. If, like every intrepid traveller, he had on his person a pocket compass, he would discover that the smaller figure, when on her pedestal, would have been facing due north towards the sea. A measuring tape would have confirmed her height as six feet. The larger, male figure faced south and stood 13 feet above his plinth. He appears to be wearing a helmet and cape, the style of which suggests it is Egyptian in origin. Fascinated by his unusual find the walker rambles on to reach his goal, leaving the area to the investigation of our witch and wizard, with their rods and a small group of competent dowsing supporters.

They set to work and quickly discover the source of the negativity. Both figures are surrounded by a complex of strong energy lines. Although a positive energy line was discovered running through the head of the larger figure, confirmed as the male, it was totally over-shadowed by the more powerful negative black-water energy running at right angles through the prone female figure. There was also strong negative energy running directly through the head and this was emitting a strongly repulsive aura which deterred people from approaching. Susy gained no permission from the rods to touch the head.

The purpose of these figures was not disclosed by the rods but while not erected at the same time they were closely related in historical terms. The female, smaller figure was the older by three hundred years, and was erected around 7100 years ago, while the larger, male figure was erected 6800 years ago. This time frame of around 5000BC, towards the end of the Neolithic period and the approach of the first Bronze Age, would coincide with the appearance of the Egyptians on the island and would suggest, along with the headgear and cape, that the figures were of Egyptian origin, a fact confirmed by the rods.

Although much had been discovered, the encounter had produced more questions than answers, as not only did the rods give no indication of the reason for their existence but neither was there any explanation of the presence, in this area, of these massive, non-indigenous lumps of rock with an approximate weight of 9 tons. And so, the questions remain: 'Why, Where from, and How?'

Travelling south-east through the village of Avtepe, a brave, or perhaps reckless, driver can coax his car up what is little more than a goat track to reach a cave set hair-raisingly high in the rocky mountainside. Abandoning the puffing and panting car on a cleared strip of flat land, the wizard followed his eager guide, another competent and enthusiastic dowser, past a large carved rock, through dense scrub towards a dangerously steep scramble and a frighteningly insecure-looking spiral staircase, which has recently replaced a vertical wooden ladder, that enables intrepid archaeologists and curious dowsers to reach the cave. According to the published legend they had found themselves at cave tombs which dated from 5–6th century BC.

While there was little to see inside the cave, apart from the remains of the burial slabs along the side walls, separated from the main entrance corridor by archways, and a dry well at the far end covered with a secure metal mesh for safety, the rods had a more interesting tale to tell.

A positive energy line ran straight down the length of the cave in the middle of the corridor. It was crossed at each archway by alternate positive and negative energy lines and where each crossed there was an energy portal. Where the portal was positive, the pendulum indicated clockwise energy and where the portal was negative, the energy ran anticlockwise. It was a site clearly chosen for the strength of its energy lines. The rods indicated that the cave had been used about 1000 years earlier than the official record. It was believed to have been built originally for the burial of noble families but was never actually finished and there was no evidence that any adult had been buried there. There was, however, considerable dowsing evidence that young people, both boys and girls, had been sacrificed within the cave, possibly to accompany dead nobles and assist them in the afterlife. This was a common practice at the time.

While the well at the far end of the cave was dry there was a strong black-water flow nearby at a depth of 56m. The rods confirmed the suspicion that the well had been used to dispose of, not only corpses, but the living bodies of thieves and vagabonds, and it was this use that had led to the cave being known locally as the 'Execution Cave'.

Although the views from the cave entrance were spectacular, it was not a wholesome place and the wizard was left with the very practical mystery of how those early people accessed the cave opening, high in the vertical face of a mountain, possibly carrying the dead weight of bodies and why they would go to such trouble.

Of course, another theory of early usage was that it was a store house, perhaps for illicit goods, and certainly there was every reason to believe that this cave could be closely guarded and protected.

Returning to the car the safe way, sliding down the incline feet-first, keeping one's centre of gravity as low as possible which meant placing most of the body weight on the backside and using the heels, where necessary, as a brake, it only then remained to encourage the little car to retrace its bumpy track to the main road and head for home.

Travelling east along the south coast of the Karpaz Peninsula, a traveller will reach the picturesque village of Kaleburnu. Situated to the north of the road and nestling against the hillside, a dowser will find it a worthwhile detour on his way to Zafer Burnu or the Monastery of Ayios Andreas.

Winding up to the village one may spot an occasional sign to the Ancient Kastros Hill Cave Tombs. The narrow road comes to an abrupt halt with just about enough room for three cars to park and subsequently turn around. The wizard led his enthusiastic followers down a precipitous staircase to the cave entrance, which, like the Execution Cave, was embedded in a vertical rock face. Clambering in over the rocks at the entrance, a couple of the more sensitive in the group hesitated and then initially retraced their steps. They were immediately aware of the very heavily negative aura of the place and instantly complained of headaches and nausea. Most did steel themselves against this and eventually curiosity overcame physical repulsion and they followed the others into the cave.

The layout of the cave was very similar to that of the Avtepe cave and it was much the same age. Here, there was definite dowsing evidence of pre-pubescent female sacrifice and burials in the hewn-out, side caverns of the cave. No-one felt good about the aura of the cave and it was, perhaps, no surprise that a number of the group experienced serious electronic interference with their camera mechanisms and one expensive camera failed to operate inside the cave. Four out of the five cameras used in the cave showed a variety of orbs on the pictures that were subsequently viewed.

The cave faces a well-known landmark, Kings' Hill, which is an acclaimed archaeological site. While the 'dig' is now closed and declared completed by the archaeologists, the dowsers believe there is much more in the area to discover. Being a perfect look-out, it was no surprise to find that it had been a Greco-Roman Fortress and the rods revealed the position of storerooms, guard-room and sentry boxes, all of which were undoubtedly known to the research archaeologists but unfortunately, not recorded on the site.

According to the rods, and not surprisingly due to the position, it is a very energetic area and was almost certainly used by many generations earlier and so may well be worth further investigation in the future.

Chapter Fourteen

– ARCHAEOLOGICAL –
RECONSTRUCTION

We have already seen that the dowsers' skills and, indeed, their rods, can be pointed in many different directions. A phone call from Dr Muge Sevketoglu, the archaeological director of the Tatlisu Neolithic Reconstruction site, opened another unexpected avenue for their talents. The extensive and culturally invaluable site along the north coast at Tatlisu was, as ever, desperate for the resources and financial support to continue the 'dig'. The site had already offered up a treasure trove of Neolithic artefacts, the remains and layout of Stone Age huts, which the team had already started to reconstruct, and animal bones including evidence of the earliest recorded cat.

Anxious to continue excavations, but conscious of the expense of false 'digs', the project director called in the dowsers to help identify the area most likely to yield 'finds'. Bob, Susy and Julie answered the call, and guided by their rods were able to indicate with uncanny accuracy an area that proved ultimately, and to the great relief and delight of the self-confessed sceptical director, to be rich in clues to the area's Neolithic past.

This initial contact led to a close association between the dowsers and the Tatlisu Project, which has now gained financial support from the Turkish Embassy and the support of the local Anglo-Turkish Association.

There have been significant 'finds' on the site of this Neolithic settlement, which dates back some 10,000 years, including numerous pre-ceramic artefacts and over a thousand shards of obsidian, the shiny, black, vitreous deposits from a volcano. (We are to meet this material again in an entirely different setting.) Analysis has shown that these particles originated in Mount Ercyes, the volcanic mountain in central Turkey, whose early eruptions were responsible for the characteristic landscape of Cappadocia with its tufa pillars, or 'fairy chimneys', which has to be one of the most readily recognised natural sites on earth.

The aim of this project is not only to extend the archaeological knowledge of this Neolithic area for academics, but to reconstruct a section of the settlement as it would have been at the time, using materials as close as possible to those that would have been used in that era. Guided tours of the current 'dig' are planned and there will be a comprehensive 'Interpretative Centre'. The whole enterprise will encourage an awareness, knowledge and respect for the local history and culture of this 'special' island, for both locals and tourists and particularly school children and students.

The dowsers are proud to have been able to use their skills to aid this exciting venture and are standing by poised to be called upon to help direct future 'digs'.

Whilst dowsing so many of these ancient sites, it became evident that the rods, when decisively questioned, could supply considerable information about the structure of buildings that may not be accessible to archaeologists and historians and so fairly accurate scale drawings and hence reconstruction became a distinct possibility.

This idea of reconstruction was also foremost in their minds when they visited the site of the 'Three Churches', along the north coastal path of Karpaz about 3km east of Ayios Filon. The ruins are at Aphendrika, the ancient city of Urania, which was one of the six most important cities on the island in ancient times. Like most historical sites there was considerable evidence of multiple overlays of occupation. The most obvious remains are 'old' rather than 'ancient', with the earliest evidence belonging to the Hellenistic Period which extended for about 300 years from the death of Alexander the Great in 323BC. The Roman Period followed, so there was mixed evidence of Greco-Roman activity.

Archaeologists have found the remains of an ancient citadel or palace and rock tombs all dating back to Hellenic times. They also discovered the remains of a harbour, now silted up and unusable.

A chance meeting with a couple of Australian tourists, who turned out to be Greek Cypriots, whose family had lived in the area, revealed the legend of a pirate-tunnel that led from the harbour and tracked underground for half a mile inland to open by a secreted entrance among the rocky outcrops. But the rods are a match for the legends and it was not long before there were whoops of success as dowsers tracked the concealed passage from the sea to its entrance in the hills. While it was confirmed that the track was used for piracy and the transport of contraband, it was not established whether the tunnel was man-made or a natural underground water course that had been carefully preserved, when it ran dry.

However, it is the three Churches that are the best preserved of the ruins. The general layout of the settlement has been well documented by archaeologists and historians. Sadly, the Arab raids of the 7th century AD badly damaged the earlier buildings. Travelling east along the track from Ayios Filon, the first Church reached which stood to the northwest of the old city square is the Church of Ayios Georgeos (Church 1 for identification). Built in the 10th century, and so late Byzantine, it is one of the most recently erected structures on the site. Beyond this to the east is the Panaghia Chrysitissa Church (Church 2) built some 400 years earlier in the 6th century. However, to the south-east of the square are the impressive ruins of the Romanesque-style Panaghia Asomatos Church (Church 3) which is the best preserved of the three. According to records the original three-aisled basilica was built in the 6th century but was destroyed a century later by the Arab raiders. The current ruins are those of a 14th century construction.

At this point the rods took over.

Whilst there was a slight discrepancy over the exact ages of the existing ruins, the rods substantively confirmed the official records, which, incidentally, were not known by the dowsers at the time, but have been researched since. However, there was strong evidence that the site had a much older and more sinister history. Predictably all three churches were located on powerful ley lines. Two energy lines run almost parallel through churches 1 and 2, on a NW–SE track. The line lying to the north was female and positive, while that to the south was male and negative. At the point where the lines passed the churches they were 3 metres apart. Further energy lines were detected through each of the churches. In Church 1 a female/positive line ran through the centre of the church in a N–S direction and was crossed in the centre of the church by an E–W line. This produced a portal with a double vortex. The direction of energy movement was defined by the witch's pendulum. When positioned over the inner vortex the pendulum swung widely in an anticlockwise direction, showing the energy being absorbed into the earth, whereas over the outer vortex the movement was clockwise and the energy was moving upwards.

The presence of these powerful energy lines suggest that the area was known from very early times and as in other cases throughout the world was probably used not only for worship but also for sacrifice.

The rods certainly became insistent in Church 2 that there had been Egyptian involvement. It has been mentioned before that while the Egyptians were not ever long-term settlers on the island they visited and traded, and it is likely that some stayed and left an influence on the culture. On numerous occasions the dowsers have found that their rods have included the Egyptians along with other early settlers. If the rods were correct, this would have been most active in the Bronze Age and would have meant that the site had been used since around 1500BC. The only supportive evidence for this theory was a psychic-emotional response rather than a practical one. While dowsing in the third church, one of the group, who was particularly sensitive to spiritual vibes, was suddenly completely unexpectedly overcome by emotion and collapsed into a paroxysm of uncontrollable sobbing. Once she had been soothed and eventually guided from the scene of her distress, Susy was able to investigate more intensely. She found that they had been working over an exceptionally strong vortex of negative energy in an area that had been used for early ceremonial, human sacrifices, and indicated that the site dated from much earlier than was at first thought.

A careful and discerning reader may be wondering why this account is in the chapter called 'Reconstruction' and they would be right to question this. As ever on these jaunts, we have strayed from the original path, but we will now retrace our steps and continue our conversation with the Australian/Greek tourists. With much hand waving gesticulation, they indicated that there was a belief that in folklore of the area, the three churches were linked around the square by overhead walkways. This at first appeared most unlikely and there seemed little remaining evidence of such a structure, apart from a few, erstwhile unexplained, chiselled indentations in existing walls. It was certainly possible that, given the modification brought about by weathering of the soft stone, these could have held cross beam supports for such a walkway. When asked, the rods were adamant that this was the case, and with their help the position and the 5 metre height above the present ground level of the walkways or bridges was determined. Using a tape measure and basic compass, the distances and angles could be determined and without further intervention by the rods, sufficient measurements could be taken to enable a skilled craftsman with interest and time on his hands to produce a plausible scale model of the square and the surrounding churches when they did indeed form the focal point of a flourishing and important city.

Chapter Fifteen

– EXTRA-TERRESTRIAL –
VISITORS?

While the various sites visited have much in common, they also exhibit their specific individual differences, and it is always fascinating, whatever the circumstances, to watch the rods so completely confirm or expand the work of the archaeologists and ancient chroniclers.

Swinging off the main road between Famagusta and Dipkarpaz towards the little village of Kumyali and parking the cars by a sign indicating a historical site, the interested visitor would notice a well-preserved, small Greek Church. The rods immediately confirm that this, apparently insignificant place of worship, is built over powerful earth energy lines. A male, negative energy line runs alongside and parallel to the outer southern wall, while a strong, positive, female line runs directly east/west through the centre of the church (nave). As the initial responses were positive, dowsers were surprised that their bodies were receiving very negative messages. Some could not enter the church, experiencing nausea, headaches and shortness of breath. Further investigation revealed a powerful water course at right angles to the church, fed by a spring some 15 metres below the surface. There was dowsing evidence that another building had stood over the spring in earlier times and it was believed that this had been a Baptistry. Although the movement of the water was producing negative energy it was not believed that this was the cause of the intensely, overpowering bad aura.

If one could disregard the odd plastic bag and discarded water bottle, the view would have been truly gentle and idyllic. Sadly, the rods confirmed that it had not always been a scene of joy.

As so often happens, the Church had been built over the site of a pre-historic, Neolithic, pagan place of worship and sacrifice. Numerous, pre-pubescent, 13-year-old girls had lost their lives, sacrificed to appease or intercede with the ancient gods. This had been encountered so often, not only on the island but also when dowsing at Gobeklitepe in eastern Turkey and on similar sites in Malta.

It was undoubtedly the spirits of these tragic young human offerings that caused the disturbing aura of the place.

Following a marked walking track, a group of dowsers came upon a cutting in the rocks. This area is known to local archaeologists and is recorded as an official site.

Here the rods are at some considerable variance with the official record.

The three cave-rooms are enclosed by two positive, female energy lines and are at a depth of 3 metres below the surface. The rooms are approached by two sets of steps, side by side, cut into the ground-rock. The staircase on the right-hand side is made up of ten steps of normal human spacing but that to the left is very different. Here the same drop and depth is covered by only four giant steps. Those that had previously dowsed at Akdeniz immediately recognised the similarity and the structure caused considerable incredulity and speculation among everyone. The speculation was only intensified when the intrepid dowsers climbed carefully down the steps and ducked under the low stone overhang at the doorway, in order to enter the rooms. The largest room ran across the bottom of the staircase at right angles to the steps. It held three long carved platforms or beds, one along each wall. These were shaped at head and foot and were at least 3 metres long. The rooms to each side were smaller but over the doorway of the western-most room there was a carving, worked into the wall. It showed clearly a head, with energy-like rays projecting from it, like a halo or aura. (It was discovered that this was not a unique motif as another was found above a similar cave-room on a northern headland some 30 miles to the west.)

The rods confirmed that the entire site was incredibly old. Both steps and carvings were given as between 7000 and 6000BC suggesting the Stone Age period, again showing a remarkable similarity to Akdeniz.

Bewildered yet emboldened, investigators used their rods to query the large steps and the use of the rooms. Many of the more sensitive dowsers found their rods very ready to impart unusual and surprising information and among them there was amazing consensus.

This is the story of the rods. The entire construction had been influenced and built by aliens. Humans had been involved but aliens had first inhabited these three rooms. The deep, wide steps had been built for reptilian extra-terrestrials and they had occupied the long room and the 3 metre beds. The smaller rooms at the sides had been occupied by a smaller humanoid species called 'the Greys'. Both species are now well accepted by those who study alien visitations, and neither are thought to have had malicious intent. The right-hand steps were also built for the Greys rather than for the humans, as had been believed at first. An experienced dowser entered one of the Greys' rooms and found steps leading down into the earth. Sadly, the flight was blocked but it is firmly believed that excavation would show that it led to further underground rooms and perhaps even an underground village like the Turkish city of Derinkuyu in Cappadocia.

This concept was supported by the discovery of two large underground water supplies held in natural cisterns, which could have sustained a village.

Later research indicated a similarity in the rock structure and an incredible likeness in the rock forms, to the vast cave city of Ellora in Maharashta, India. This, in turn, has been likened to Derinkuyu. The main differences would appear to be in sophistication which would be expected when the accepted age of Derinkuyu and Ellora falls towards the earlier part of the 1st millennium BC, whereas Kumyali is believed to be much older. However, two striking coincidences are marked. If the rock surfaces of Ellora are viewed carefully they appear to be of the same geological structure and have been carved in a very similar way to the supporting blocks and beds in the cave dwellings of Kumyali. There is also a very strong suggestion that in some way extra-terrestrials were involved in Ellora. The evidence is two-fold. The massive rocks have been carved out into passages but, while the surface of the rocks is smooth, the tunnels they form become so narrow that it would be impossible for a human being to move between them in order to carve them. Some tunnels are only 1ft wide and take right-angled turns. Sections of the stone work are decoratively carved with figures, invariably in three layers. The upper layer, almost certainly, depicts the gods. Below them are definable human shapes, but on an even lower level are the cave dwellers and these take the form of smaller humanoid shapes and low lying, narrow-bodied reptilian and snake-like creatures. These are not intended to be seen as animal shapes and are generally considered to be depictions of alien, intelligent beings.

Alien intervention on a number of sites dowsed, had been strongly confirmed by rods that, in every archaeological case, have been proved accurate. Subsidiary support for this theory occurred when rocks have been discovered with fine cut surfaces that show no signs of chisel marks and the rods have clearly indicated that the cuts were made by lasers, a technology far beyond that presumed available at the time of construction.

The dowsers believed that, in Kumyali they had stumbled on something quite extraordinary, and it had provided them with much scope for research and food for thought.

Moving on, reluctantly, from this fascinating place they soon discovered two stone pools, again cut cleanly into the rocks. The smaller of the two was only just over a metre deep and dated from the earliest Bronze Age. The second was much larger, five metres deep and had been constructed nearly a thousand years later. Both were fed by natural springs and initially there was considerable debate as to their function, whether they were water storage cisterns for an ever-increasing population, or bathing pools. However, the more sensitive dowsers were aware of an overpowering feeling of dread and as they continued to question their rods, the wizard gave them a quizzical smile. He had seen these before and his dowsers would see them again. He knew what they had been used for and it wasn't nice.

They were undoubtedly the blood-letting tanks that some had already seen at Akdeniz.

By now, there were a number of the committed dowsers, who had faithfully followed our witch and wizard on several expeditions, and had undoubtedly received from their rods confirmation, on more than one occasion, of the presence or intervention of 'alien' or 'extra-terrestrial' beings. Of all the areas investigated this was, without doubt, the most difficult to explain or prove, and so for most dowsers the hardest to accept. Over this the witch and wizard were unable to help. They had no problem, themselves, as they believed their rods implicitly, but never-the-less sought to increase their knowledge of sightings, and surfed the web endlessly for information. They knew that pyramids, across the world, had always been associated with ancient mysteries and even their very structures had led to questions about their origins and purpose.

Pyramids have always held a great fascination for archaeologists and mathematicians alike. Much has been written about the mystery concerning the Great Pyramids of Giza and certainly the very shape of the pyramid, with its square base and four faces pointing directly to the heavens has given rise to much speculation regarding its mystical properties. The fact that the pyramids are not unique to one time or culture is significant. They have been found, not only in Egypt, but also in Mexico, China, the Indonesian Islands and many other places, not to mention Dr Sam Osmanagich's controversial Pyramids of Bosnia.

It may at this point be helpful to mention some of the researched facts which have led to the awe surrounding pyramids generally. The Great Pyramid of Cheops or Khufu in Giza has long been acknowledged as one of the wonders of the world. It was thought that, on construction, it stood 146.5 metres high, but with erosion its present height is 138.8m. Composed of 2,300,000 individual blocks of limestone and granite rock, its weight is almost 7 million tons and its footprint is 13 acres (Wikipedia). The means of construction alone has caused massive research and experimenting over the ages and even today no definitive conclusion has been reached. Many theories abound, but when other hidden factors are taken into account none of the ideas yet proposed seems adequate. The mathematics of the structure leaves the uninitiated spellbound. It is, for example, accurately aligned with the earth's true north to within less than one degree. Its dimensions derive from the cardinal dimensions of the planet. (A constant of 43,200, is used in calculations and relates to the key motion of the earth.)

"The accuracy of the dimensions indicates space age precision and strongly suggests a lost civilisation." Ref. Graham Hancock.

This may well indicate the intervention of extra-terrestrial superior intelligence being responsible for, or influencing, the work.

The Bosnian Pyramids have been declared by some to be fakes, promoted to enhance the morale of a flagging nation after the Balkan war of the 1990s. However, our witch and wizard have met Dr Sam and were much impressed by his research, enthusiasm and vision. Susy has visited these pyramids in Bosnia and is totally convinced of their authenticity. Having employed her rods, she was able to confirm that the structures are sited on powerful energy lines and that there was an intense aura of positivity in certain areas that she strongly believes to have healing powers. Again, like the pyramids of Egypt, which we know to be 4500 years old, the Bosnian pyramids exhibit evidence of highly advanced technology, far beyond that available at the time of their construction. The air inside the vast structure is fresh and replenished and yet there are no conventional air shafts to aid convection. Instead there is a complex series of undulations in the roof of the underground tunnels which causes a steady movement and circulation of air. The building material, while concrete-like, has been found to be four and a half times stronger than any similar material known today. In spite of numerous analytical tests in various countries no definitive explanation has been given for this phenomenon (Dr Sam Osmanagich). And so, again, we find pyramids associated with the presence of unexplained advanced technology.

By now many of you will be questioning what this has to do with our subject, so I will continue.

If you should find yourself on the road through the mountains behind Karsiyaka take a sighting from the top of Selvitepe, the highest peak in the Kyrenia Range, south-west to Olympus, the highest point in the Troodos. Slightly to the east of a line between the two peaks and conspicuous on a wide flat plain, you will spy Cyprus's own pyramid. Although this has been visited by Dr Sam, who acknowledged a number of similarities between this smaller pyramid and his Bosnian Pyramid of the Sun, there is no evidence that this has been investigated by local archaeologists. Even from a distance our witch and wizard knew that there was much more to discover than met the eye. Remote Viewing suggested that the construction was very old indeed, dated at 12,000BC, which would put it before the mini Ice Age. Closer investigation with the rods confirmed, as expected, that it was situated on a massive conflux of powerful ley lines. At least twelve lines entered the pyramid crossing at the centre of the base. Some proved to be positive others negative, while some were male and others female. However, it is believed that male can change to female according to the solar cycles.

Uncannily aware that this was not an ordinary place, the rod-questioning became more intense. This is the story of the rods. About 400 metres to the west of the pyramid there is what can only be described as a track. (While clearly defined by the rods, it is, of course, invisible to the naked eye. This immediately suggested a similarity to the much larger and well-documented Nazca lines of Peru, an area which is constantly the centre of new research and reports.) The Selvitepe–Olympus track is energised and draws its power from the energy lines of the pyramid. The function of the pyramid is as a marker and charging point for alien transport. The track is an alien flight path. Re-charging is related to phases of the moon and takes place between March and July and during October. At other times the energy emission is closed.

Unlikely as it sounds, it should be possible to detect these energy emissions with the appropriate electrical meters and even measure their strength.

Undoubtedly birds and animals would be aware of this energy and even use the lines for navigation. Certainly, cranes and pelicans on their annual migration have both been observed travelling directly in line with the main track.

(The dowsers' findings provoked some challenging questioning. If they were correct and they had, in fact, discovered evidence of extra-terrestrial visitors to our planet, could this possibly lead them to a better understanding of some of the phenomena that they had observed – the giant steps, the long stone beds, the smooth-cut stone devoid of chisel marks, the huge statues carved in rock from a different area and many others?)

Fascinated by their findings and fired with the enthusiasm to prove them correct, our witch and wizard devised a plan. Just as a crescent moon was rising over the horizon and the daylight faded, a little car was seen scurrying up the mountain side. By the time it reached its narrow parking spot on the south-facing side of the mountain it was already dark. Bodies tumbled out, silhouetted against the mountain, dragging sleeping bags. Minutes later, snug in their bags with their beanies pulled well down over their ears, they were enjoying their first mug of hot chocolate from their ever-handy flasks. The silence was all-pervading, apart from the occasional eerie screech of an owl, and the steady throb of a commercial airliner overhead, droning its nightly way to Izmir or Istanbul. Behind them was Selvitepe and way below them on the plain they could just make out the outline of the pyramid. As they lay back against the hillside and scanned the dark sky the anticipation was electric. Would this be the night they had dreamed of? Would they, actually, see a UFO and even perhaps an extra-terrestrial?

They both knew people, normal, sane, balanced people who vowed they had seen them. Surely, if anyone was to see them, it should be them! They stared upwards into the dark void until the odd star appeared to change colour or dance around but not even a satellite passed overhead.

The long night wore on. The rocks beneath them began to eat into their bones. Their feet went to sleep. They ran out of chocolate biscuits and the street lights in the village below twinkled relentlessly producing an unexpected level of light pollution.

By 2am discomfort overcame their earlier enthusiasm and they agreed mutually that this was not the night that they would meet ET so sadly they rolled up their sleeping bags and crept home.

However, in spite of their disappointment on this occasion, they still fervently trusted the results of their dowsing and believe they just picked the wrong time and that someday they would be rewarded with a sighting.

Chapter Sixteen

– TALES FROM ACROSS THE POND –

Although Bob was well known among his long-standing friends in Canada as a highly competent water dowser, a skill much prized in a country where so many live, in remote areas, far from the town water supply, it was not until he moved to the south shore of the province that he became involved in more mystical experiences. It was not long before he was being called upon, not only to dowse for wells and lost treasures, but invited to tea because people felt their homes had a special 'aura'. He soon found that he was experiencing similar domestic situations to those he had seen in Cyprus. One house he visited was enclosed by two positive energy lines and the happy owners declared they had always loved it and had long vowed never to sell, even though they lived and worked far away in the USA.

He was called to investigate a commercial building. The distraught proprietor had only recently taken out a lease, and within a week of opening the expensively appointed business, everything seemed to be going wrong. The staff complained of feeling ill. They were not turning up for work and when they were there were discontented. Bob turned up for a preliminary check. Even on entering the building he was aware of very strong negative energy. He quickly identified three very strong black-water courses. Two were running through and alongside the property, parallel with the adjacent main road. The third ran at right angles to the road, crossing it and passing straight through the centre of the building and so crossing the other negative lines. While the negativity from these lines was certainly strong enough to produce the symptoms which were being exhibited, Bob sensed that there was more to discover. In one room he had a strong sensation of death. Using his rods, he ascertained that he was at the scene of a brutal murder. After the murder the body had been dragged across a landing and thrown down a flight of stairs. When he reached the door to the stairs he found it locked. When he questioned the proprietor, she told him that none of her employees would go near the stairs, let alone walk down them. They all maintained the place was evil and they were afraid, and so the door had been locked to give them protection. Bob was concerned that the door was also a registered fire-door and so actually the employees were putting themselves at risk. Anxious that he had the support of his witch he promised to return as soon as possible with Susy. Susy was aware of the repressive atmosphere as soon as she passed through the street door. They immediately set to work on the main cause of the problem, the strong negative black-water on both sides of the property. They worked together to divert two of the flows into a nearby stream but the other ran very near to a neighbouring building, so they attempted a new technique, and using their combined power, forced it into the ground. Checking with the rods indicated that the malignant energy had been removed.

Susy also confirmed the details of the horrific murder and so Bob bravely unlocked the staircase door and descended the stairs. At the bottom, he used all his psychic energy to remove the negativity left by the murdered spirit. The employees were told only that the problem had been dealt with, and the fire-door was left open. The staff returned and business continued.

Bob was not confident that the new procedure they had used to remove the one line would be permanent, and so he was extremely pleased when he returned a couple of weeks later to find the proprietor all smiles. The staff had returned happy and supportive and the business was thriving. There was no sign of the black-water and there was a general air of positive optimism.

It was at a supper party that a very sceptical neighbour invited both Susy and Bob to visit his land and tell him what they could about its history. He would give them no clues and was clearly testing them. The elevated land was beautifully located with wide views of the surrounding countryside. Even on their approach they were aware of early First Nation activity. It had undoubtedly, at one time, been a settlement and Bob found no less than four separate burial sites. Meanwhile Susy was delving into more recent events. She had discovered the spot where a house had once stood. Relying on her powers of premonition to direct her questioning, she ascertained that the house had been destroyed by fire. Bob was able to confirm this. Their rods then led them through the story. It was in the very late 1800s and there had been a small hamlet in the area that even included a tiny church of which there was no longer a sign. It was the burnt-out house that attracted their attention. A mecca for all the drunkards and brawlers of the area, it came as no surprise to find that the house had acted as the distillery for the local moonshine. Then, one night, an unexpected tragedy occurred. Perhaps the revelry had been particularly rumbustious, and someone had been careless, but, whatever the cause, it was never revealed. At the height of the carousing, the still exploded, killing one man and engulfing the house in flames.

It is not likely that one event would completely change a person's beliefs but, in this case, the extremely shocked neighbour had to acknowledge every detail of their findings correct. The story was well known to him, being part of his own family's dark and secret past.

Bob was about to leave Canada and return to Cyprus when another unexpected case presented. A friend, over lunch, shared his concern over his tenant. The young man with a wife and young daughter had taken a job locally and moved into the area some months earlier. Before the property had been rented the owners had comprehensively re-decorated and re-furbished it but the wife, sensitive to earth energy, had not been happy with the 'feel' of the house. Shortly after taking out the lease the tenant began to suffer strange symptoms. Among the more severe was a sudden propensity to stutter. He also complained of general debility and muscle spasms in his leg that caused him to limp and experience tingling in his feet. He believed that the cause of all his problems was an allergy to something in the house, perhaps a mould. There has been considerable publicity recently about the serious health risks of exposure to certain damp-moulds in property. Bob agreed to visit. Ironically he arrived with the owner to find the tenant's wife sick in bed and heard the young daughter had developed an undiagnosed, face-disfiguring rash that resembled impetigo, or perhaps measles. It was, altogether, a sorry situation.

The tenant welcomed the wizard into his home and seemed keen to co-operate, obviously anxious to have his condition improved.

Bob first identified a flow of black-water that ran alongside the house about two metres from the outer wall, passing the office and the kitchen. He then surveyed the back of the property and found a very strong, 3-meter-wide black-water stream flowing down through the property at right angles to the original stream and straight through the living room and the kitchen. It crossed the original line about a metre beyond the kitchen wall producing an extremely negative portal which was certainly close enough to affect the occupants of the house. Before he took any remedial action, Bob then decided to check out the cause of the tenant's ailments. The rods immediately confirmed that his problems were not caused by an allergy, but they vigorously blamed the black-water. However, Bob also checked out his diet and found him deficient in certain minerals which could be easily replaced by increasing the green vegetables in his eating habits.

The next task was to find some way to ease the offensive stream away from the property. Devoid of his wizard's staff, Bob borrowed a broom from the tenant, and went to work. Going out into the road he tackled the narrower line first. Here he was able to re-direct it a few feet until it was running in line with the road and so would not affect other properties. He used both his scribe and the owner, a newly enlisted dowser, to verify, first the initial position of the line and then the final resting place away from the house and along the roadway. Satisfied that he had at least destroyed the damaging portal, he decided to take a closer look at the stronger line. He immediately realised that to divert it in the normal way would be impossible as it ran too close to other properties. He, therefore, decided to employ a technique which he and Susy had only recently perfected and he used his staff to send the malignant energy into the earth. Again, both the scribe and the owner confirmed that it was now safely embedded and away from the property.

While there was no doubt in the wizard's mind that the main cause of the tenant's family's problems lay in the individual's proximity and sensitivity to the effects of the negative energy, he also had a sneaking suspicion that in the tenant's case there was a subsequent psychosomatic effect and remained very curious to hear a future report of the situation.

Although there had been a passing reference to the First Nation, Bob and Susy had little idea then, the extent of their future experience with these fascinating indigenous people.

This started with an unexpected connection with Cyprus. Usually friends, knowing only of Toronto and Vancouver, expressed total ignorance of the far eastern province of Nova Scotia. It was therefore a great surprise and quite remarkable, when, on hearing of our wizard's intended destination, a friend exclaimed excitedly that her best friends from working days in Azerbaijan had retired to the Province, and "wouldn't it be great if you lived near them!" As Nova Scotia is the size of England and Wales combined, the likelihood seemed remote, but obviously a meeting was written in the stars, as it transpired the couple lived about 20 miles up the coast – practically next door in Canadian terms. The coincidence did not stop there as they soon discovered that they even had homes built by the same bespoke builder.

The following summer, contact was made and there was an immediate rapport with this delightful couple. Jim, who in his working life had been a senior executive, in a very down-to-earth business, turned out to be highly sensitive to the paranormal. In his retirement he had developed the hobby of short story writing and for his writing group had written the tale of his grandmother's haunted house and the ghost which he had seen himself. He was immediately interested in Bob's acumen with the rods and enlisted his support. It transpired that on his daily stroll through his extensive woodland with his old and much-loved hound, they encountered a spot on the path that caused both man and dog some discomfort. Always at the same spot the dog would hesitate, tremble and begin to whine. At exactly the same point, Jim reported that he would feel a chill even on the warmest day and the hairs on his arms would stand on end. Would the rods be able to shed some light on this strange phenomenon?

The wizard, fascinated by the possibilities, raced to his car for his rods and, duly armed, the three took to the woods with the faithful rods akimbo. Eventually Bob began to feel the tell-tale vibrations in his hands through the rods. Just as the rods began to cross the dog began to whine and Jim confirmed that they had reached the exact location. It was now up to the rods, through the wizard's careful questioning, to divulge something of the history of the area. And so, the story was revealed.

During the mid-18th century, there had been a series of battles in the area. The region had been colonised by the French for over a century but now the British were challenging their rule. The First Nation, the original inhabitants of the area being the Mi'kmaq tribe, fought alongside the Catholic French Acadians to repel the British invaders. It was during one of these skirmishes that a group of Mi'kmaq had been slaughtered at the very spot that had been identified. Although the bodies had been removed by members of the tribe for traditional burial rituals, it appeared that the spirits, presumably incensed by the invasion, and intent on defending their land, had lingered at the place, reluctant to leave and take the 'three-day road' to their eternal rest.

As so often happens, a chance encounter opened a door to another unexpected experience. It was while Bob was dowsing for a well on a Canadian neighbour's land that the neighbour, also a sensitive dowser, suggested he meet a friend of hers who had a remarkable property nearby. She made the introduction and in due course, Bob presented himself at Maria's house, armed with his doughty rods and accompanied by his faithful scribe and a fascinated independent witness.

Maria was baking when they arrived but welcomed them warmly and, rapidly rubbing flour from her hands onto her apron, she followed them into the delightful garden, anxious to see what they would find. Bob lost no time in raising his rods and striding across the driveway towards the perimeter path. Suddenly to the consternation of the three observers he stopped dead, as though he had walked blindly into a brick wall. He staggered backwards as though being physically pushed away, which is exactly how he described what he had felt. Every trace of colour drained from his face. He was clearly 'in shock'. Recovering rapidly, he immediately realised he was in the presence of very powerful forces and he had stumbled into a closely guarded area. He humbly asked the rods again for permission to enter, and this time he was allowed to slip cautiously through the barrier into the mystical world beyond. He said it was like creeping through the wardrobe into Narnia or, indeed, sliding down the rabbit hole.

Although immediately aware that this was a 'special' place, he had no idea at that time the wealth of discoveries that lay hidden beyond the rods and which would become gradually unfolded over a period of years. Some findings were later endorsed and graphically depicted by evidence from Maria, herself.

The initial view of the garden was a sheer, natural delight, with an abundance of 'old-fashioned' flowers. The ubiquitous and indigenous lupins vied with delphiniums for space, while giant sunflowers and hollyhocks towered over them. An abundance of variegated hostas edged the pool, affording shelter to the frogs and toads.

Once inside the invisible wall, Bob's eye was drawn to an attractive rock feature to the left side of the lawn. Approaching with the rods, it was immediately confirmed that the rock marked the position of an energy portal. Maria then admitted that she had been visited some time earlier by a dowser from another part of the Province. He had also become very excited by the spot and suggested that she mark it. She had subsequently spent many hours touring garden centres, far and wide, in search of a rock that she felt was just right. Suspecting that this fellow dowser must have known more about the local history and the earth energy, Bob hoped to arrange a meeting. Sadly, before the meeting could be fixed, he heard that the chap had died. And so again, Bob was thrown back on his own resources and undaunted he pursued his investigation and at the same time scrolled Wikipedia for information about the history of the area.

He started his practical survey, by identifying the 6 energy lines that crossed at the portal, thus showing 12 energy lines radiating from the centre point. He also discovered that these lines were overlaid by major ley lines which bore closer scrutiny. (He was to discover numerous portals throughout the property, which was to prove more 'highly energetic' than any property he had seen before or since.)

Maria then showed him to another area on the far eastern side of the garden. This was an enchanting spot where a little bridge crossed a small brook feeding a pond, in which Maria kept a few gold fish. It was shaded by tall trees and the trickling water gave a peaceful and tranquil feel. There was a little patio where one could sit and relax and soak in the aura. Maria, herself highly sensitive to the extra-sensory perceptions, believed this place also had powerful positive energy, which Bob was soon able to confirm with the rods. It was, indeed, another portal, but this time it held such high positivity that it seemed to emanate certain beneficial effects. Maria was so convinced of this that she admitted that she always stood jugs of her drinking water in the shade there, in order to absorb the natural earth positivity. She also related a tale which she believed demonstrated that this portal had healing properties.

A couple of years previously she had been introduced to two travellers, and this was their story.

They were two old friends from another Province. The one had recently been given the terrible news that she had an inoperable and terminal tumour. With the prospect of only a short time to live, she was seized with a desire to see once more her childhood home in Cape Breton, Nova Scotia. She asked her friend to accompany her and they set out to make the two-day drive. Once they crossed the Province border it was a straight road to Cape Breton, so neither could ever explain what suddenly took them on a three-hour detour to the south shore. Finding themselves in a strange town they stopped at the first guest house and asked for accommodation. Unfortunately, there were no vacancies but as it was getting late in the evening the proprietor suggested that they try the neighbour who may have a spare room. With some trepidation they approached the door but were soon put at ease by Maria's warm welcome.

The next morning over breakfast Maria listened to their sad story and as they were tired after their long journey she suggested, without explanation, that they rest in the garden and that the lady with the tumour should sit by the pool, over the portal.

Later the cancer sufferer, who had spent several hours relaxed by the pond, admitted to feeling a powerful pulling force, upwards through her body, and then a deep sense of peace. She thought no more of it, believing that the sensations were merely due to her body gradually relaxing after the stress of the previous few weeks and the long journey. Finally, they went on their way to fulfil her dream.

It was some weeks later when Maria received a surprise phone call from her earlier visitor, to thank her for a miracle. Happenstance had driven the two friends from their planned route and deposited them in an unknown town. Another stroke of chance had carried them to Maria's. They had eventually continued their journey with warm memories of their stay with Maria. The patient appeared happy and relaxed as she re-visited the scenes of her childhood, but it was with inevitable dread that she visited her oncologist on her return home.

However, she found her doctors totally baffled and they could give her no medical explanation as to why, after three weeks of tiring travel in another Province, they could find no trace of the malignant tumour that should have killed her. They could only suggest that some miracle had occurred, as they had never before witnessed such a recovery.

Inspired by this story, Bob encouraged a dear friend, who also had been diagnosed with stage 4 cancer, to relax by the pond. Again, a deep sense of peace and renewal was reported and while, in this case, sadly, it did not cure the advanced systemic cancer, it doubled the life expectancy given by the doctors, and gave the patient a deep sense of inner calm that helped him cope with his condition.

◆—◦—◦—◆

Realising immediately that there was much to learn in the area, Bob was delighted to accept Maria's warm invitation to visit whenever he could, to continue with his investigations.

Arriving early one morning, he was surprised to see a young girl sitting reading in the garden. He recognised her immediately as he had known her for many years, but as she lived in the city some 60 miles away, he was astonished to see her at Maria's. He sat down with her and they shared experiences. She told him that she had met Maria some years earlier when visiting the town, a well-known beauty spot. Since then she had been aware of the 'special' aura of Maria's garden. She believed that it was because of her Caribbean heritage that she was particularly sensitive to the aura and she could give no other explanation of why she was always drawn there at times of stress, or when she just needed to self-regenerate and escape from her busy life as single mum and teacher. Bob explained that he was, at that point, investigating the ley lines and she said she was aware of the energy, even without rods, and led him unerringly to another portal in the woods just beyond the garden boundary.

This was only one of many instances that Bob uncovered where people with psychic and mystic sensitivities had found themselves drawn towards this extra-ordinary place often for no obvious reason or purpose. Most could only explain it as being guided to a spiritual renewal, to their psychic Mecca.

Chapter Seventeen

– ORBS, SPRITES –
AND FLOATING SPIRITS

Still musing on the unexpected encounter, Bob continued with his survey. To his amazement he discovered that one of the main ley lines running through Maria's property was the very line that he and Susy had identified crossing Baspinar Plateau in Cyprus. It was travelling from the Mayan Pyramids, passing through all the major buildings of power along the eastern seaboard. It travelled along the coast of Nova Scotia passing through Oak Island, the legendary site of Captain Kidd's treasure (although none has ever been found and many have lost their lives seeking it), and across the Atlantic, taking a northern sweep across Iceland and then down through Europe. Each stage was noted, and the route first identified at Baspinar was confirmed by the rods.

The number of other major ley lines indicated without doubt that this was a very 'special' place. (Later, together with Susy, Bob would discover that the number of portals in the surrounding area was at a concentration that they could never have imagined and had never experienced, even on the highly energetic Baspinar plateau.)

The energy levels were to be confirmed anecdotally by Maria who was taking a keen interest in their work. She admitted to them that in 2003, when she was first drawn to the property she had little understanding of the psychic or mystic worlds. She was a deeply thoughtful and sensitive person who understood the principles of yoga and the ability to raise one's level of consciousness by meditation, but she knew nothing of cosmic energy, orbs or sprites.

However, she, herself, was to witness some unusual experiences which would change her perspective. Over the first few years she had a number of unexpected callers that she came to believe had been sent to her to tell her about the energy around her. She felt a close affinity to the Mi'kmaq people and believed that there was some connection between the energy she was being told about and the early First Nation. In 2008 she had a Mi'kmaq friend, a native teacher from Thunder Bay, living nearby for several months who guided her. During this time, she met a local Mi'kmaq man, the son of the local Chief, who came to her, saying that he had received a message to make her a drum. He presented her with the first and only drum he ever made. This gift left a remarkable, lasting effect on her and she has continued to attend drum ceremonies and even welcome them in her garden. When her visitors began to talk of the healing powers of her portal she invited a Yogi from India who gladly expanded her knowledge of earth energy and spiritual healing.

She sees life now as a spiritual journey and as in the story of the Marten which I will share with you later, she seeks guidance from her spiritual grandmother in the tradition of the Mi'kmaq culture.

She had received many guests over the years and some had been privileged to witness the energy of the place. It is rare that earth energy is revealed visually but on numerous occasions, different visitors, at different times, from different places had, on their return home, sent Maria amazing digital photos taken in her garden. There was a barbecue in the garden and on warm summer evenings friends would gather to cook their burgers and enjoy the company. Pictures would be taken to record a memorable evening. But what a surprise some had when they viewed their pictures! A number showed orbs, which admittedly, some disclaim as light defects in the camera, but it is strange that several different cameras should malfunction at different times only in that particular place. Some photos showed very rare light effects with light sprites flashing out of bushes and another showed one bush with red light behind it just as one might imagine the 'burning bush' in Sinai. This may be dismissed as a fluke, but it is indeed strange that, over a period of time, so many people, unknown to each other, should experience these phenomena at the same place, when they have never seen these effects before and have considered it sufficiently significant themselves that they made a point of sending their photos to Maria.

<hr>

On one occasion when our witch and wizard had finished their deliberations for the day, Maria, who had been watching their progress with interest, called them into the kitchen where she had her laptop already switched on. She had mentioned previously that many of her visitors over the years had sent her photos that they had taken in her garden. Most of the 'snappers' had no idea that they were surrounded by a spectacular display of energy phenomena.

I feel I must add at this point that there will be, perhaps many, readers who will dismiss the following as camera faults, dust particles and unusual light effects. That is as may be, but it has to be noted that these photos were all taken within ten square metres of each other; they were taken by a range of people unknown to each other and over a period of years. The examples that I am bringing to you are merely representative of the many more that Maria has received. Some of the photos are reproduced here; for others I will attempt to describe the observed phenomena along with the comments of the senders.

This is the story of the visitors.

In 2009 Maria sent an orb-decorated photo of her daughter and family to Diana Cooper (author of 'Enlightenment through Orbs'), for her comments. Diana marked a spot on the picture and returned it with the response, "This is a portal, and some are orbs".

And so, Maria's journey into the unknown began.

In 2008 a young Danish researcher took a photo of friends in Maria's garden and sent it to her as a keepsake. It would be three years before Maria noticed the rods of light in the upper right-hand corner of the picture and thought they may be significant. Not having met our witch and wizard at that time, she sent off both the pictures of her family and the one she had received from her young Danish friend, to a well-known dowser and mystic, for her interpretation of the pictures. This is her reply.

The first photo (daughter 1 and family): "The orb in this photo is the spirit of Jack, your daughter's grandfather and he is also one of her spirit guides".

The second photo (daughter 2 and family): "The orb beside E (granddaughter) is her guardian angel but is not the spirit of your mother E".

The 'rods of energy' were described as a 'chain curtain of 'iron': "Our dowsing told us that this is a 'curtain' of energy, like a highly concentrated mass of energy that is the marker of a portal".

In the same year, 2011, Maria received a picture from two ladies who had sat around the barbecue chatting. An orb can be clearly seen directed at one of the women. No explanation was given at that time.

In June 2012 a photo arrived with a large and distinctive orb obliterating a guest's neck. Her accompanying message stated, "I will hold on to my interpretation of this as a hug and visit from my mom's spirit".

In April 2014, a bizarre message arrived from JN, a recent guest. "We stood under the energy and saw a being – 10 feet tall – its hands resting over us".

Just one month later from CL – "here is basically what happened when I was standing in your garden in the portal of energy. My eyes were closed, and I was just noticing my sensations and energy and started to feel very tall. I almost felt like some giant person. I opened my eyes and looked towards the trees in the back and saw that out of the small forest came many, many people, men and women, I don't remember whether there were children. They were all looking at us. They were brown-skinned, long, dark, smooth hair. They were dressed in leather-coloured clothes. It was very calm and peaceful. I felt a connection between them and the trees, almost as if they were one. Then the vision was gone".

In the summer of 2013 the local Music Group were fortunate to catch a renowned Irish, Gaelic, a cappella choir on their seasonal tour of the eastern provinces and arranged a concert at the local church. These highly skilled and finely tuned songsters produce a haunting sound imbued with all the magic of their Celtic heritage. Their perfectly blending tones and gentle modulations raise the hairs on the back of the neck and transport the listener to a mystic land. Staying in the town for a few days it was not surprising that news soon reached them of Maria's rather 'unusual' garden. Intrigued, the leader of the group arranged to visit. Himself a true Dubliner, friend of leprechauns and kisser of the blarney, he was immediately aware of the magic of the place and agreed to return the next afternoon with members of his choir to sing for Maria and a few friends. All the singers were enchanted by the aura, and the music they made was truly sublime. All too soon the experience was over and after a few photos were taken, they were off to their next engagement. When Maria looked at the photos, she was barely surprised to see the misty cloud above the group. As a photo taken just before the group arrived had not shown anything unusual, Maria was convinced that what she saw was the spirit of an angel, or what she called an 'entity' travelling with the group to take care of them. She sent the picture to the choir leader with her explanation and she, at least, was not surprised by the response.

"Whether I believe it or not this is a wonderful and comforting thing. What you don't know is that the girl with the red hair directly below the shape has recently (I mean last week) suffered a bereavement of someone close to her".

There were other pictures, like the one taken in 2012 of the purple flash, but, in that case, the explanation given at the time by the orb-interpreter was so esoteric that even our wizard doubted its content.

Anxious to satisfy himself, he dowsed the copies of the photos, by then in his possession.

He quickly ascertained that in the first picture that had received no explanation, the energy directed at the women was a positive, protective force which emanated from the guardian spirits of the deceased First Nation. He was to learn later of the negativity that may otherwise have surrounded them. Similarly, JN's giant man and CL's swarthy hordes were confirmed to be native spirits, always around for guardianship and protection.

The purple light in the bush, the white light shooting up the bird-feeder, and the 'stair-rods' of light were all different manifestations of energy, related to nearby portals, either cosmic energy entering a portal or earth energy leaving it.

And so, the saga continues as photos in this area continue to be produced with effects seen in few other places. However, we must now move on.

Chapter Eighteen

– INTRODUCING –
THE FIRST NATION

Having been somewhat familiar with the history of Canadian First Nation tribes for nearly half a century, and knowing that in earlier times the area had been inhabited by the Mi'kmaq, Bob suspected that they would have been well aware of the energetic properties of the spot he was working on, and would have used it to their advantage. The Mi'kmaq people have a deep spirituality, which goes back for thousands of years and has an intimate connection with the land. Although the actual name of the tribe was not recorded in history until the mid-17th century, the tribe belongs to a vast generic race, the Anishinaabe, that incorporates many other North American tribes and has a history that dates back 6000 years, although there is evidence of the presence of the original First Nations 5000 years earlier.

The earliest First Nation tribes had a highly developed life-style and there is evidence that they travelled across the vast area that is now the United States and Canada, not only following food but also from as early as 8000BC up until 500AD trading in obsidian, that black, vitreous volcanic material, so prized for cutting tools and arrow-heads and found in vast quantities in Wyoming.

(The perceptive reader will remember that thousands of small pieces of this material had been found on the Neolithic site in Northern Cyprus, and were believed to have been used, not only for tools, but the small pieces were used as currency.)

The Anishinaabe, which means 'good humans', believed they were on the right road to the Great Spirit. Their homeland was called Turtle Island where the Great Spirit was created from divine breath. The individual tribes were differentiated at the Council of the Three Fires in AD 796 but the Mi'kmaq name did not appear until 1676.

They worship Kisu'lk, the Great Creator. Central to their tradition is the concept known as 'Msit No'Kmaq' or 'all my relations'. It is a belief in Animism, the idea that everything on earth has a living soul. This means that animals should only be killed if there is danger or a need for food, and plants should only be harvested for a purpose. When another living spirit is killed or harmed, then an offering is given (usually tobacco, which carries a spiritual meaning) in thanks for the sacrifice made.

They believe that the spirit has been sent to learn, to heal and to be improved. Those already in the spirit world watch over those on earth. If the goal in life is not accomplished the spirit is returned to earth to try again. Only when they have achieved success do they remain in the spirit world and guide others.

They believe that death is part of the cycle of life and they have no concept of Hell. They believe that a soul which has repeatedly been evil will just cease to exist.

They demonstrate their traditions through rituals and ceremonies. Dancing, songs and epic poetry play a large part in these ceremonies but perhaps the most significant is their use of the drum. They believe the rhythmic beating of the drum represents the heart-beat of Mother Earth and as it also reflects the sound of the human heart it reinforces the relationship between Man and Nature.

It very soon became clear that, just as other places of worship, Maria's garden, so rich in powerful energy lines, was believed to be the site of an original Mi'kmaq ceremonial area and a key part of an ancient settlement. However, it soon transpired that it was dated much earlier than the differentiation of the First Nation tribes and was therefore associated with the rituals of the original Anishinaabe.

From earliest times, long before colonisation and the iniquitous herding of these sensitive people into Reserves, the tribes had wandered freely, seasonally following their food. During summer months they would travel to the coast and set up their extended family wigwams, some large enough to hold fifteen people. Here they would fish, collect shellfish and grow crops while the weather stayed warm and the days were long. But when the nights became chilly and the days drew shorter they would abandon their summer settlements and move inland, where they hunted moose and caribou.

Convinced that he had stumbled on the site of an ancient summer settlement and excited by his discovery, Bob set to work to investigate the extent of the site and note its dimensions. He had started with the boundary that had initially denied him entry. He followed the wall around, at times scrambling through the edge of an adjoining wood and at one point slightly encroaching on the neighbour's garden but eventually he had described a neat rectangle and had the measurements for the perimeter. Needless-to-say, the two portals were well inside the enclosure. He then set about locating the actual Ceremonial Hall. However, dowsing at this level is extremely tiring and it would not be until the following year, when he was joined by his witch, that the work continued.

Meanwhile, Maria had followed the discoveries with enthusiastic fascination. Although trained as a scientist, and, generally, scientists are not renowned for their ready acceptance of the mystic, Maria proved to be the exception. She had always felt a strong affinity to the First Nation and was drawn to their art and culture. She had many Mi'kmaq friends and the local Chieftain would invite her to the great annual Drum Ceremonies which she always found intensely moving. There was a strong indication that somewhere in her past there was a First Nation ancestor from whom she had undoubtedly inherited a powerful sensitivity to the spiritual and mystical. She knew that her garden held a powerful aura and she was not surprised by the First Nation connection. She was totally convinced that when she had moved across the country some years earlier, she had been 'guided' to this special place. She knew she was meant to be its guardian.

Further dowsing enabled the witch and the wizard to identify two distinct ceremonial areas, to define their boundaries, and also to date them. The smaller rectangle surrounding the healing portal had been constructed in

2800BC while the larger one whose perimeter bordered the garden dated from 2200BC. The rods confirmed that both had been built and used by the Anishinaabe. Just as Bob had initially found when encountering the outer border of the larger rectangle, so he discovered the inner, older area was also closely psychically guarded. He then set to work to create and mark out an entrance 'gateway' to each of the defined areas.

Even without the use of his rods, Bob was conscious that he was in the presence of extreme earth energy. So far, all the energy had been overwhelmingly positive. Both portals were clearly positive, but he knew there was more. He strayed beyond the garden into the tangled woods behind the house. It took him little time to identify three more strong portals. Investigation with measuring tape and ropes soon showed that they were in a straight line and, obviously, related energetically. While investigating these portals, his senses became attuned to other sensations. He had the premonition of death. Taking out his rods he discovered that he was walking over a burial ground of much more recent history. It was dated 260 years ago and was of Mi'kmaq origin, thus suggesting that the tribe had continued to use this area over the centuries – perhaps their summer camp, as was originally believed. Questioning the rods more closely, he discovered that the many graves were separated into those for men and those for women. Each grave held four bodies. Some deaths were caused by smallpox, one of the greatest killers of native people, or diphtheria, another lethal European import.

(He was thrilled and excited when, a year after making his discovery, he met a member of the Mi'kmaq tribe who happened to be visiting Maria at the same time, and she confirmed for him that the burial ground was, indeed, known and recorded in the Mi'kmaq annals.)

Just as they believed they had exhausted the information available to them, Bob suddenly had a strong sense of intense evil. He, like everyone who had seen them, had been fascinated by the number of pictures that had been taken which showed energy effects. Studying the pictures again he realised that they had all been taken in the same part of the garden and that they were all near the barbecue. He strolled over to the marked-out area and, as he approached it, was overcome with nausea and knew instinctively he was on the site of unthinkable slaughter and mutilation. He did not share this information with Maria for fear of upsetting her. Not wishing to proceed further at this time he decided to wait and confide in his witch. They both agreed that this must have been an earlier happening and could have no connection with the Mi'kmaq settlement they had been investigating. Unlike early Europeans, Greeks, Romans and Egyptians, there was no record of any human or animal sacrifice, throughout the history of the Mi'kmaq or Anishinaabe. Such activity was totally against their beliefs – rather, there are many legends in which animals offer themselves as sacrifices but only in relation to feeding humans. Such a tale is that of the Marten.

On a cold autumn morning in a low valley, a great grey stone lay covered in dew. The very old stone had lain there for many moons and seen many seasons and animals pass by, but on this day as Niskam heated the rock and the dew rose from it, Niskam decided to give it life. As the rock became hotter and hotter and the dew formed a mist above, it was given the body of an old woman. This was Nukumi. Kluskap (first man) had been watching the birds, plants and animals and learning all he could. One day he travelled into the valley and met Nukumi. As he talked to her, he realised how wise she was, and he wanted to learn more from her. She told him she was happy to be his grandmother and share her wisdom, but as she was an old woman she needed meat to survive. She could not live only on plants and berries. Kluskap called to the marten swimming in the river and asked if he would give his life so that his grandmother could live. The marten agreed to do this for his friend.

For this sacrifice Kluskap agreed to be the marten's brother. So Nukumi killed the marten and placed him on the ground but Kluskap felt so bad he called on Kisulkw to return the marten to life. Now Nukumi used her wisdom and also spoke to Kisulkw and the marten was brought back to life to return to the river. But where he had lain was the body of another marten. Nukumi told Kluskap that from that point animals would be brother and friend to Kluskap. They would be willing to provide food and clothing, the necessities of life, but must always be treated with respect.

It would be inconceivable that a People who could recite such legends and sing of such beliefs could ever have committed the atrocities that Bob had uncovered. So, witch and wizard questioned their rods and found they were on the spot that had been used as a sacrificial area 4500 years ago. This was the time of the Anishinaabe, but like the later Mi'kmaq, they respected life and would not have committed such atrocities. The rods confirmed this and gave no indication that this was the work of the First Nations and at this point they left, mystified. However,

Susy could not clear the vivid image of the mutilation and organ removal from her mind. She remembered the stories in the newspapers of the dreadful and unexplained horse and cattle mutilations and the many conspiracy theories that surrounded these horrible events. She decided to put one more frightening question to the rods. Unable to reconcile their findings with the First Nation history that they knew, Bob delved into Anishinaabe culture and legend and found that their earliest records indicated that the tribes had a belief in the 'gods' that came from other planets. They affected an affinity with superior beings that they believed to be extra-terrestrial.

Meanwhile Susy had returned to Maria's to ask her question.

"Was this mutilation the work of extra-terrestrials?"

The rods went wild, immediately confirming the presence and activity of an alien race who had associated with the Anishinaabe and had carried out the mutilations for experimental purposes.

Though shocked themselves by their discovery, they need not have been fearful for Maria, as she was so confident of the positive protection that surrounded her. She fervently believed that the sprites and orbs that had been seen on the photos sent to her and the visions that other visitors had clearly seen, were all manifestations of positive and protective spirits there to counter-act the evil which had been perpetrated by the invaders. She felt she was invulnerable to the past and was being watched over in the present and would be protected and guided in the future.

The following winter she sent what she believed was further evidence of this.

On Valentine's Day an email arrived in Cyprus with a short greeting and a picture of Maria's garden attached. The garden was covered with a deep layer of snow but there, described in the middle of the grassy area between the two portals, was a huge and perfect heart. The heart was totally isolated with no markings leading to it from any point. Looking more closely at the picture it was clear why Maria had sent it. The outline of the heart had been marked out, not by humans, but by the hooves of a deer.

Chapter Nineteen

– FURTHER FIRST NATION –
ENCOUNTERS

As so often happens one experience, and hence tale, tends to meld into the next. Bob was still in the throes of investigating her property, when Maria invited him to breakfast one morning to meet her friend, whom she said she had met through a strange chance a few years earlier. The friend, Dina, who had a stressful job in a busy American city, had been in need of a completely restful holiday. She was still grieving the loss of her closest friend and had suffered a number of physical and emotional illnesses the previous year. In her own words she was "exhausted; body, mind, and spirit". Realising that she had to take charge of her life, she had enrolled in a Yoga Therapy Course, and after 10 days had returned home re-vitalised, her mind teeming with plans, and keen to start on her schemes. Her husband, however, believed she needed more time, and planned to give her a holiday treat, but on her own admission she was reluctant to travel at the time. In spite of this he began looking for suitable places to visit. At first, he had little idea of a destination that might encourage his wife to join him. Then, among the welter of brochures and literature he had acquired, he spotted Nova Scotia.

They had never been to Nova Scotia before and he was enchanted by the pictures of gentle scenery; the rolling green hills, the rocky coastline and appearance of pastoral calm. It could not have been more different from their noisy, crowded city life. He made his decision and eventually he persuaded Dina that she would enjoy the change. He has no idea to this day what led him to Maria's town and to a guest house nearby.

They met Maria, one day, at a local coffee house, started talking and immediately struck up a friendship. Dina, who was very familiar with faith healing and was highly sensitive to the mystic, found instant rapport with Maria.

On visiting Maria's home, she was immediately aware of the powerful earth energy present and as soon as she arrived was drawn to the little pond, where she sat gathering in the healing energy of the portal and watching, fascinated by the antics of the frogs.

(She would confide in Maria later that some time earlier she had seen a vision that involved a frog and that had lingered in her mind. Well versed in mystic culture, she knew that the frog is a totem of metamorphosis. Some say that frogs facilitate a connection to the afterlife or symbolise a bridge to another chapter of one's own life. This she related to her own life, which was in turmoil at the time, and considered it possibly a message, or sign.)

Dina and her husband fell totally in love with the area and visited again the following year renewing and deepening their friendship with Maria. Ultimately, they decided to take early retirement and move to Nova Scotia, as so many do, captivated by the gentle charm of both its scenery and its people.

It didn't take them long to find a property further down the coast with a delightful view of the bay and although the house needed some renovation they were soon packed and ready to move in.

It was now three years on from their first visit when Bob sat down to breakfast. He was immediately charmed by Dina, whom he found attractive and highly sensitive. Maria had related many stories about Bob's dowsing skills on her property and Dina was enthralled. She invited Bob to visit her and her husband, as she felt there were factors at their new home that would bear investigation. She was quite coy and gave him no details, so Bob was intrigued and arranged to visit for coffee at the first possible opportunity.

He found the beautiful, old colonial house easily. Standing a little above the lane, which crept along a headland, it had magnificent views to the east across a wide bay to the open Atlantic. While he was still chatting to his new friends, his scribe, who invariably accompanied him on these jaunts, had wandered off with her own rods. Having taken a good look around and knowing a little of the history of the area, she felt certain that the 'investigation' would lead to First Nation connections. With little confidence of success, she walked across the driveway in front of the large garage which was a short distance from the house, trying to connect with the Mi'kmaq spirit and to her amazement she had a violent and positive reaction from the rods. She raced back to the house to report her finding. On hearing her outburst, the owner, Roy, turned pale and even the wizard looked impressed. Apparently, Roy, a businessman, whom no-one would expect to believe in ghosts, had just been nervously relating to Bob an experience he had some months earlier when they had first moved into the property. He was anxious to make it quite clear that it happened in a morning, on a clear day (eerie mists can often drift in from the sea) and he had most definitely not been drinking. After breakfast, he left the house and walked towards the garage, as he approached he saw a figure near the garage door. He vowed it appeared touchable but, as he went to call out, it faded away. The vision left a photographic image in Roy's mind and he was able to recall the appearance in great detail. He looked a tall man and from his dress it was obvious that he was a First Nation chief. He proudly rode a powerful and arrogant horse and wore the full ceremonial dress of the tribe including the eagle-feathered headdress. Later Dina also admitted that she had seen this vision.

The fact that even the scribe had picked up the vibes at exactly the spot was remarkable and certainly confirmed that the whole area was highly energetic.

It soon became obvious that Dina was aware of, and highly sensitive to, the energy in the house and that she also could sensually distinguish between positive and negative energy. While it was generally a delightful property she felt the negativity in certain rooms and believed it responsible for some health issues that they had both suffered.

And so, with a number of clues already before him, our wizard set to work with enthusiasm. He quickly discovered a stream of black-water, a metre wide, flowing through one side of the house and straight through the kitchen, which was undoubtedly the cause of at least some of the negativity felt in that area. While in the kitchen Dina would experience a swaying action, which made her feel unwell and she had difficulty standing there for any length of time.

With his wizard's antennae at full twitch, he was convinced that this was not the real cause of the problems. He picked up the death of a woman in the living room, but this had occurred at the spot long before the house was built, so again, he did not believe that this was the major source of negativity. However, on entering a ground floor shower room, he felt suddenly light-headed and nauseous, and knew instinctively that he had stumbled on a deeper cause for concern. Suspecting that there was a link here to the vision by the garage, he questioned the rods carefully. The response was unmistakable. He was standing on the very spot where the Mi'kmaq chief had died. Although he now believed he had identified the cause of the main negativity, he was not, at the time, able to remove it. But he knew who could and she was due to fly in (by courtesy of Air Canada rather than on her broomstick) in just four weeks' time.

In the meantime, Bob toured the surrounding land. Surmising that the Chief would not have been far from home, he started to search for the settlement. Behind the house there was a gradual slope, and, covered with undergrowth, he discovered the remains of an old well. The rods were unequivocal. He was on the site of a Mi'kmaq summer settlement and the well had been the water supply for the tribe. The site had been the summer camp for the tribe for many generations. But, spiritually the area was completely deserted. There was no sign of the tribe and yet they certainly had been there. Moving back down the slope towards the house Bob received the first indication of what had happened to the tribe. He came upon a burial ground just beyond the boundary of the settlement. Close by, he found a second burial site. He was able to determine that one was for females and the other for children. On the far side of the property he found a third site which held the remains of the males of the tribe. All appeared to have died over a very short period of time which led him to question what had caused the deaths and whether it had been a battle or disease. He checked the date and found that the last tribe to settle there had been effectively annihilated towards the end of the 19th century. Further investigation showed the tribe had been wiped out by a disease, a rampant killer at the time, typhus.

Europeans arriving in the Americas exposed the First Nations to diseases which they had never before encountered and so had no natural antibodies to fight them. Such diseases as measles, smallpox, yellow fever, typhoid, typhus and diphtheria, were unknown at their arrival and set off the largest depopulations in history. This dated back to the arrival of Christopher Columbus in 1492 and John Cabot in 1497, but these visits involved only very small numbers.

However, in the mid-18th century when the French and English were battling for control, large contingents of Europeans arrived in Canada often carrying the diseases, mainly typhus, which was sweeping Europe. In 1746 France had sent a large flotilla of warships to re-take Port-Royal in Acadia. Of the 3150 soldiers aboard 1270 died at sea and another 1130 died in Bedford basin, the port of Halifax. Typhus hit the Mi'kmaq of the region hard and more than a third of the First Nation population died.

Many more may have died from a deliberate and evil act of biological warfare. In 1763 there was a movement by the French, powerfully supported by the Mi'kmaq tribes, to rise up against the British Rule. There is written evidence that the British attempted iniquitous action in an attempt to counter this movement. It has been reported that Sir Jeffery Amherst, a well-known name in Nova Scotia, suggested to Colonel Henry Bouquet that smallpox be introduced by infecting blankets given to the First Nation they were fighting. He wrote "You will do well to try to inoculate the Indians by means of blankets as well as to try every other method that can serve to extirpate this exorable race". While there is no evidence that Bouquet carried out the act it was recorded that later the same year down in Pennsylvania, William Trent wrote of a meeting with two members of the Delaware Nation, "We gave them two Blankets and a Handkerchief out of the Small Pox Hospital. I hope it will have the desired effect".

Whether in the first instance the suggestion was carried out or in the second instance it was effective, it is certainly true that European diseases killed 75% of the Mi'kmaq Nation.

Returning to the newly discovered burial grounds, the dowsing rods indicated that the demise of the tribe had, in fact, been typhus, which turned out to be in accordance with subsequent research. Bob then sought to identify individual graves, but he was now confused. He found that the rods were not indicating the usual oblong shapes but while the graves were of different sizes appropriate to adults or children, they were in fact square. For a time, he could not understand this phenomenon but then he realised that the bodies were in fact buried in a sitting position and all were facing towards the sea and the rising sun.

A moving moment of discovery and certainly more than enough dowsing for Bob in one day!

Susy was barely off the plane when she was whisked off to explore the mysteries of Dina and Roy's home. Together they decided to tackle the negativity in the hope of giving the owners peace of mind. They started on the black-water in the kitchen and planned to turn the line away from the house. This proved highly successful and removed all signs of debilitating or detrimental energy.

Then, they moved on to the shower room, where both were immediately aware of pressure being exerted on their bodies. As was usual for Bob, he felt it in his legs whereas Susy felt she was being pushed around and hassled. She also experienced a sensation in her right ear and, as so often happened when she was under stress, a panicking feeling that she was underwater.

Susy then confirmed the death of the Indian Chief and his horse, both lying near the foundations of the house, beneath where the shower now stood. The rods suggested he had died in 1829 and so he belonged to a generation earlier than those buried in numbers due to typhus. The Chief was 38 years old when he died. He had two sons, but they, and his wife, had died earlier from an outbreak of typhoid. The Chief, however, had survived the typhoid epidemic and appeared to have died, along with his horse, as a result of an accident. The rods clearly indicated him falling from his horse.

Witch and Wizard agreed that the only possibility of breaking the negative pressure affecting this area of the house was to create a positive energy circle around the shower room with a clearly defined gateway to free the Chief from this enclosure, giving him freedom and respect.

Realising that the negative forces in the property were putting incredible stress on Dina and Roy's relationship, our 'energy blasters' decided they must act quickly. Gathering together a group of empathetic friends, they went to work to create the positive circle in the manner previously described. Susy communicated with the spirit of the Chief and gradually guided it through the gateway and on its way to peace.

Susy also confirmed the death of a French lady in the living room. This did not overly concern or surprise Dina as she had seen a vision of a lady in a white gown with white hair and believed she could have been the original owner of the house. Further investigation showed that the woman had died of exposure or hypothermia during a particularly cold February, but sadly they neglected to check the year.

The removal of the negative forces in the house had an immediate effect on Dina and Roy. She later reported that she could spend hours standing happily in her kitchen indulging her long-time love of cooking, without a trace of the previous vertigo or nausea. Similarly, Roy admitted that they could both relax and feel comfortable, if necessary just doing nothing, whereas before they felt agitated and could not settle. He also said it was great to be able to enjoy a shower and even walk about the house without shoes, which he had never felt able to do before.

Certainly, the dowsers felt confident that they had removed the negativity and had identified positive energy in the house from which the owners could draw strength, and increase their own innate positivity.

However, the postscript to this tale is sad. Unfortunately, during the period of their tribulation the two had grown too far apart and other personal concerns mounted, causing a final rift, with Dina returning to her original home and family. She believes her departure had the blessing of the frogs and she tells the story of her farewell visit to Maria's, in her own words.

"The day we were to leave, one of the frogs assumed the exact position on a piece of driftwood as in my vision. He remained there as I leaned in close to place a special stone near the wood. And he remained there as I offered a special prayer of gratitude and offered a gift of tobacco… As (we) turned to leave, the frog hopped off, as if to tell us it was time to go".

Chapter Twenty

– LINKS WITH THE LEVANT –

It was again at Maria's that Bob first met John. They were soon to discover that they had many interests in common and became firm friends. Although from another Province, John had paid regular visits to Nova Scotia to research for a novel he was writing. As his fascinating book included research on the activities of the Knights Templar, of whom many legends have been told, Bob was immediately interested. Over a couple of years, they travelled together to a number of sites and shared information and findings. During the winters when Bob was in Cyprus and John, often travelling, they would keep in touch by email from time to time.

Then, one day Bob received a remarkable letter with a request. The letter contained details of a dream that had been experienced by a close friend of John's in which he was thought to have featured. The dream was not only vivid but enigmatic and disconcerting and the message arrived with a plea to both Bob and Susy to Remote View the meaning.

Jean was a warm, motherly lady. People-spotters, over their Costa in the airport lounge, would likely have her down as a 'Child Care Officer' or a 'Primary Head Teacher'. She gave no outward indications of special psychic powers and yet she was highly sensitive to the mystic. She admitted that, over the years, she had experienced vivid and insightful dreams, or even premonitions. It was after one of these dreams, that she sent her plaintive message to her friend John.

On the previous night she had suffered a particularly forceful and impelling dream. She described it as horrific in content and horribly bloody, but she said that while obviously upset, she was not frightened by the spectacle. There was no doubt, even in her waking mind, that the subject was John, but that she was also there. She was also well aware that the time was not the present.

As John, himself, could shed no interpretive light on the dream he had forwarded her account to both Bob and Susy for their independent explanation and comments.

While flattered that their skills were recognised and appreciated by people that they had known for so short a time, and excited by the prospect of having the opportunity to extend those skills into a new area, they admitted later that they had both anticipated finding that the dream was merely a replay of some long-forgotten trauma. They were both well aware that the conscious mind is capable of blocking out traumatic experiences, which may remain buried in the subconscious, to be kicked back to the surface, often as dreams, by some catalytic trigger. In this case, they felt sure that Jean was reviving a long-subdued scene of some horrendous accident, which would account for the blood.

They felt that it was unlikely that the man was John but was some man, unknown to her at the time of the trauma, who resembled John sufficiently for her subconscious mind to super-impose him on her former experience.

Without any pre-discussion and working completely separately in different buildings and at different times, both witch and wizard attempted to remove all distractions from first their physical environment, and then their own psychic consciousness. Using their remote viewing skills, they stretched deeply into their own mystic energy and then, using their friend John as an intermediary, they each managed to access his friend Jean's subconscious self. They each worked laboriously through the stages of the dream, making notes as they progressed. They checked, first the date of the event, and immediately realised that their surmise had been completely wrong and that the dream had a far greater significance than they could possibly have imagined. Eventually when each was satisfied with his and her results they reported their findings independently to your chronicler. As on previous occasions, their findings were astoundingly similar. They each confirmed that both Jean and John had been present in the dream and the dream was a recall not just from an earlier experience but from an earlier life, when they had met in a far land in very different circumstances. Bob reported that the events had taken place in Haifa, Susy said Acre, the main port in Haifa Bay, on the coast of what is now Israel. Bob gave the date as 1189, whereas Susy gave one year later, 1190. Susy had clearly seen a fortress, while Bob had described a castle. What they had both visualised was the fortress, which had been built by the Hospitalers some 70 years earlier. At the time, neither had seen pictures of ancient Acre or even had a clear idea where it was. The location and time revealed that the events had taken place during the Third Crusade. Mixed groups of European Crusaders were besieging the city of Acre where Saladin's Muslim troops and civilians were trapped. Fighting was fierce and continuous, and it would be another year before Philippe of France and Richard the Lionheart arrived with their forces to take the city, with heavy loss of life.

Jean had been a nurse working with the Hospitalers and she must have witnessed horrendous sights, as men were carried in from the battlefield to benefit from the simple care they could be given in those days. John was a Templar who had travelled with the Crusaders from France. He had suffered a deep and penetrating stabbing and was bleeding profusely when he arrived in the hospital tent. Susy reported that she had, herself, experienced an excruciating pain in her left side when that part of the dream was revealed to her.

Jean was excited to hear the revelations from her dream and confirmed that the report resonated with her emotions at the time and the impression the dream had left with her. She was interested to hear that she had known and helped John in a previous life and marvelled that fate had brought them together in their present lives.

No-one who heard of John's previous existence was surprised that he had been a French Templar. Even in this life over 800 years on, or something like 250 generations, he is still French – well, French Canadian, and so a francophone. Even in this life he has the piercing eyes, the long, straight, lean features and chiselled jaw of a Mediaeval Knight. Ironically or even, perhaps, understandably, many moons before he had any inclination of a personal connection, he had shown intense interest in the history of the Templars, researching their activities in Canada and across the globe, for his book and the presentation of documentaries.

In the light of Jean and John's subsequent reactions to their report, both Bob and Susy felt that their findings by remote viewing had been fully vindicated.

Chapter Twenty-One

– VIKING HORDES –

So often new lines of investigation come from unexpected sources. Such was the case with the Vikings.

Bob had, for a number of years, followed with sceptical interest the many stories about his local Oak Island. It was said to be the site of Captain Kidd's treasure. It was claimed that the Templars had hidden the Holy Grail in the depths of the well on the island or, if not the 'Grail', at least some of their immense wealth, secreted when they became outlawed by the Pope and the King of France in 1307. Some thought that a deep shaft on the island had been a store for the treasure of pirates and privateers over the ages. It was even suggested that Marie Antoinette's jewels had been smuggled out of England, and buried on the island, shortly before she was beheaded in France in 1793.

Ever since three young boys found a few artefacts on the island in the 18th century, the place has been a site of mystery and research. Records have shown that parts of the shaft had been booby-trapped and some have even lost their lives in the hope of discovering riches. Certainly, carvings of Masonic symbols, thought to date back to mediaeval Templars, have been found, but no-one has categorically vouched for their authenticity.

Unexplained deaths, strangely constructed booby traps, inexplicable carvings and no discovery of treasure, have led to the legend that the island is cursed. It is certainly a widely held belief that the mediaeval Templars and the early Masonic orders were heavily involved in Black Magic. Even present-day dowsers would acknowledge that those skilled in the psychic arts could put an energetic protective layer around an area and so prevent anything within it being discovered. Our own witch and wizard have exercised similar energetic powers to protect property from dangerous negative energy and we are already aware that Susy is able to block another dowser from finding what he seeks.

Could this be the source of the Curse of Oak Island?

Recently an old brooch with a ruby-type stone, and what appeared to be the hinge from an old trunk, have been found, but their origins have not been proved.

Local legend also mentions the early presence of the Vikings on the small island. This will undoubtedly come as a surprise and be vehemently denied by those who fervently believe that North America, the New World, was discovered by Christopher Columbus in 1492. However, there is considerable archaeological evidence that Europeans, certainly the Vikings, arrived in Newfoundland much earlier. Two early sagas or manuscripts are available to historians. The one, which is believed to have been written down about 300 years after the events, records stories that had been kept alive in the folklore. From this we learn that the Vikings were competent boat-builders and explorers and had ventured abroad as far as Iceland, where some had settled. By 985AD they had already reached Greenland and were ready to explore further afield. Archaeological evidence proves that shortly after this they had built a settlement in L'anse aux Meadows in northern New Brunswick.

Stories are still told of Oak Island, books written, and the research continues. At the time of writing, a TV series 'The Curse of Oak Island' is being made and a privately financed research team has brought in heavy duty machinery to delve deeper into the shaft.

Our doubting wizard, not content with the various reports from the many researchers, took himself off to the island with his rods in hand. The rods denied the presence of any treasure. Also he was unable to obtain any clear evidence of the earlier presence of either Templars or Vikings.

Somewhat deflated by his findings, he still felt that the general area had a tale to tell, and so it was no surprise when he was accosted by a couple of friends and asked if he had "seen the stone?" These two hardy Scots had tramped the trails and beaches of the area, summer and winter, and had left no stone unobserved. The stone in question was huge but being on a beach inaccessible at high tide and barely accessible at low, it went largely unnoticed. Listening fascinated to their description, Bob was determined to find it. As it happened, his son, Steven, was staying at the time and so father and son set off together on a quest.

Realising that they would have little chance of finding it by walking the beach, they decided to try to assess where a track might lead from the road, giving the nearest beach-access to the stone. They drove slowly along the road and could find no tracks. When Bob decided they had travelled too far, he turned the car reluctantly, disappointed that their search had proved in vain. However, as they slowly retraced their way, they saw a young deer standing firmly in their path, as if pointing into the hedgerow and woodland. As they cautiously approached the deer ran off, but exactly where it had stood, they saw a narrow track which neither of them had noticed before. It was dark and forbidding in the trees but Steven, convinced that the deer was showing them the way, insisted they turn on to the path. They must have driven nearly a mile at a snail's pace with Bob anxiously aware of the overhanging trees and their threat to his car's paintwork. Eventually the track opened out into a small clearing, and there half-hidden in the trees and a pretty, old-fashioned garden, stood a quaint iron-stone cottage, for all the world like a gingerbread house.

Concerned that he may be thought trespassing, Bob approached the front door and was immediately warmly greeted by the owner. He apologised for the interruption but explained his mission and inquired whether they had heard of the stone. "Oh, you mean St George and the Dragon!" was the instant response. But Bob knew instinctively that it wasn't that. "It's on our beach, I'll show you!"

They were led through the garden and down a small path to the rocky shore and there, in front of them, standing alone on the beach with its lower part submerged by the rising tide, was a huge stone. It was well embedded and looked to have been in situ for many, many years. As they scrambled towards it they saw clearly the distinct runic markings on the land-side of the stone. This was their first sighting of a Viking rune-stone. Our wizard, of course, was carrying his rods and so was soon engrossed in a preliminary investigation of age and authenticity.

This was the story brought to him by the rods: Firstly, there was no doubt as to the stone's authenticity. It was no modern-day hoax. It had originally stood high above the water line at the time the runes had been formed. This was dated at 1195AD and the carving was done in the October of that year. Three people had been involved in the craftmanship; one was the runic designer, who was joined by a master carver and his apprentice son. It took father and son 7 days to complete the work. Oddly the rods indicated that no chisels had been used in the carving but, inexplicably, a technique which employed heat, had been used to cut into the surface of the rock. This suggested a level of technology far beyond what we would have expected at that time. Gradually, over time, winter storms, high seas and ice erosion brought the stone on to the beach, above the tide-line by 1920. The stone was eventually reached by the tide and its base is now lapped every day. Fortunately, or even possibly strategically, the carving faces inland and is therefore protected from the major, eroding ravages of the sea. Like an iceberg, with most of its mass underwater, so the rune-stone has 3 metres of stone buried beneath the surface of the beach.

Although quite exhausted, there was just one more thing Bob felt he must check. There were, indeed, four energy lines running through the rune-stone where it presently stands. These cross in the middle producing a powerful energy portal. Armed with so much information and a warm invitation to return, Bob and Steven returned home tired but satisfied and excited to start on their own runic research.

Unfortunately, they were unable to pursue their practical investigations until the following year. However, in the meantime, Bob had heard a claim that the carving was recent and had been chiselled by a teenager. He, never doubting his faithful rods, found this hard to accept and determined to gain confirmation of his discoveries. He did agree that it was remarkable that such a striking stone had remained unnoticed for so long but realised, on reflection, that all signs of the carving would have been completely hidden for centuries by layers of mud and algae. Clearly this had been carefully cleaned away over recent years. As there was no indication when the carvings were actually revealed, he believed it was possible that the petroglyph was discovered by chance and when the inscription was clear, the discoverer either claimed to be, or was taken for, the inscriber.

The following year, without supplying any advance information, he took Susy and two more experienced dowsers to see the rock. They followed their normal procedure and reported their findings independently to your scribe.

The dowsers' results were remarkably similar, and all were adamant that it was an original rune-stone. Susy had the carving dated at about 1200AD and confirmed Bob's previous finding that a father and son were the carvers with a third male in attendance most likely the designer. She also confirmed that the work was not done by chisel but by some form of heat or laser. Susy believed the stone had moved three times but had been in its approximate present position for about 600 years, though the tidal-flow had changed over that period.

At the time neither Bob nor Susy knew anything about the legends of the rune-stone, but both found that there was an association with death. Bob found that the stone had been carved to commemorate the deaths of 9 people including a leader. He suggested that they had been approaching from the sea and had drowned. They had been washed up or dragged ashore and buried on land. Susy found a burial site just above the high-water mark. She had nine or ten burials including a man wrapped in a blue cloak that she believed was the leader, in whose honour the stone was carved. Her rods also suggested that the stone was a grave marker.

Investigation of the bank above the shore confirmed that there had been a small, if only temporary, Viking settlement around the turn of the 12/13th century.

However confident the dowsers were of their findings it all sounded most improbable. The highly sceptical recorder was driven to research. Two glaring questions presented themselves. The first and obvious one was 'Did the Vikings actually reach Nova Scotia and if so, what were the circumstances?' The second question was more challenging to a mind that had been trained as a scientist. 'If the rods indicated, as they clearly did, that the carvings had not been made with a chisel, and there certainly were no chisel marks, but had been produced by some heat process comparable to a modern laser, how could that possibly have been achieved at that time?'

The careful reader will, by now, perhaps, have started to make connections. He will remember the smooth-cut stones around the door-ways of some of the ancient sites visited. The long stone bed-like structures at Kumyali that were perfectly smooth with no signs of tool marks. Your scribe had seen similar smooth hewn blocks at Machu Picchu. Could there be a connection?

Tackling the first, and perhaps the easier, question first she turned back to the Viking sagas. The second of the sagas was left to us by Leif Ericsson, a Norse explorer from Iceland, who is now widely believed to have been the first European to set foot in the Americas. Ericsson was born around 970AD and died about 1020. In his writings he describes how the Vikings travelled from Iceland to Greenland and on to a land south-west of Greenland, which they called Vinland. This was almost certainly Newfoundland. Here, some settled growing wild grapes, eating salmon and building ships out of animal skins. He records descriptions of Viking encounters with indigenous people, undoubtedly the ancestors of the Mi'kmaq.

Although, by the middle of the 11th century the Norsemen are moving closer, they are still a long way from where our dowsers found their rune-stone. However, the Vikings were always doughty seafarers and fearless explorers and they would not settle in one place for long. By the start of the twelfth century they had travelled south-west along the coast line of Nova Scotia and it is believed that Vinland then extended as far south as Cape Cod. Even a cursory glance at a map would confirm the likelihood of one of their early skin-covered ships being blown off course by Atlantic waves and taking refuge in one of Nova Scotia's protected bays or wrecking on its rocky shores.

The location of the rune-stone, on the western shore of a south-facing bay, made it highly likely that at least part of its history had now been revealed.

Over the last four years others have 'discovered' the stone and a considerable amount has subsequently appeared on Wikipedia. It has now been officially called the Norumbega

Vinland Stone, and the carving has been identified as a representation of the Ramsund legend. This first appeared on a stone in the Swedish Province of Sodermanland. The stones were built, usually by aristocratic families to commemorate their dead and to form a bridge from this life to the next. They were generally called 'Bridge Stones'. Similar stones dating back to Norse times have been found in parts of Britain. The carving depicts Sigurd, the dragon slayer, the forging of the sword, and roasting the head of the dragon. The horse, Grani, can be seen by a tree in which sit the birds, who warn Sigurd that the smith intends to kill him. The decapitated smith is found beside his bellows and hammer, while Sigurd himself is under the dragon on the right of the carving.

This is only one of the many Norse legends that have survived and have inspired so many writers and musicians over the years, not least Wagner and Tolkien.

Pictures of the stone were sent to Professor James Knirk at the Museum of Cultural History at the University of Oslo. Although he, like others, believes that the carving may be a modern copy, some of the information that he provided was very interesting. He reported that some of the original legend was missing, possibly, he suggested, because the stone was not big enough or that some of the stone surface was washed away. However, he also acknowledges that although the runic inscriptions are somewhat modified, the depictions are true enough for the runes to be read. According to the professor it reads "Sigrid made this bridge, the mother of Alrik, the daughter of Orm, for the soul of Holmgeir, the father of Sigrod, her husband".

The question of its age and authenticity still looms large in the academic world but at least over the past few years it has been acknowledged and listed among other rune-stones around the world and certainly our dowsers remain totally convinced that it was a Nordic hand that inscribed it over 800 years ago.

The second question posed was not so easily answered. It would be possible, perhaps, to dismiss the problem by denying the rods and yet everyone had seen the difference with their own eyes. The surfaces were completely smooth and there certainly were no chisel marks, and why should the rods give a false response to this when they had been so uncannily accurate on so many provable occasions.

Puzzled and frustrated, both witch and wizard accepted that their rods would yield no further information and therefore it was time to move on.

Chapter Twenty-Two

– FACT OR FICTION? –

The scribe, however, was not satisfied. Looking back over the records it became obvious that every time the rods reported the use of heat or laser-type techniques to produce smooth surfaces, they also indicated that this was 'alien technology'. This came as no surprise to either witch or wizard as both believe that there is considerable evidence from earliest times that there were periods in history when archaeological records of Man's achievements indicate he had knowledge and skills far in advance of those expected at the time. They attribute this to intermittent intervention from superior intelligence from other planetary or solar systems.

Bob, if challenged, will quote people he knows and trusts who have claimed to have seen aliens, been close to landing alien craft, been 'taken up' or abducted by aliens, and even chipped by aliens. He believes that extra-terrestrials have somehow visited earth and have not only brought knowledge and skills, but have in some cases integrated with humans and so this strain is carried genetically. He will use the rods to determine what percentage of alien genes a person carries.

If this were proved then it would answer many of the unanswered questions posed by archaeology; however, it was all a step too far for the doubting scribe. Then, still delving deep into alternative research there was a minor breakthrough.

The Nazca tracks in Peru, already mentioned as claimed extra-terrestrial runways and landing sites, were again in the news. A tomb was found nearby with six mummified bodies which were carbon dated as 6500 years old. While they were 'humanoid', having 46 chromosomes, there were genetic differences and notably they had alien-shaped heads and only three fingers and three toes. Professor Konstantin Korotkov from the Russian National Research University declared "they could be aliens". Ref. Jon Austin, The Express, Mar 12th 2018.

So, maybe aliens did visit and stay; however, this begs more questions than it answers. Where did they come from? Is their physiology like ours, or do they have the ability to instantly adjust to our planetary conditions? How did they get here? Do they de-materialise to cover vast distances and then re-materialise?

An increasing number of eminent physicists and planetary scientists are conceding that in our vast Universe, ever expanding as knowledge increases, it is logical to assume that we are not the only form of intelligent life. If this is acknowledged, then we must also accept that there may be forms of intelligence far more advanced than ourselves. As yet, we do not know, we can only surmise.

Shortly after this revelation, another piece of information presented itself and at least produced corroborative evidence of structures that had been observed and tested by the dowsers. In Brian Foster's series 'Third Phase of the Moon' he covers a fascinating archaeological survey in Peru. A team of professional archaeologists working on Inca buildings and ruins in Cusco and Machu Picchu discovered that some of the megalithic works that had been catastrophically damaged had, in fact, been constructed over even more ancient sites, which showed clear evidence of advanced, high technology. They displayed seats carved out of rocks with no signs of chiselling and no sharp corners. The edges appeared routered, but there were no tool marks. They exhibited photographs of stone architraves that appeared as smooth as modern moulded plaster or polystyrene. The team reported that the surfaces were so smooth it appeared the hard stone had been turned into toffee, moulded into shape and then re-set. They also questioned how this was done and amazingly mentioned the possibility of laser or, more probably in this case, sound waves, to produce the effect. They declared it was as though matter itself had been manipulated and the rock turned to putty. This brings to mind the Bosnian Pyramids and Dr Sam's reference to the concrete-like material that was so many times stronger than present-day concrete. It certainly echoes the findings of our dowsers and the reports of their rods.

The archaeologists in Peru also noted that the levelling-up was better than in modern buildings and the megalithic bedrock was within 1% of level, in spite of being in an earthquake zone.

The rods' regular confirmation of extra-terrestrial technology intensified the wizard's interest in possible alien intervention. He began searching the internet for information and records of possible sightings and encounters. Increasingly, it became the central feature of his dowsing and enthusiasm. All the evidence he was accumulating seemed to be leading him along one track, but he still was without the proof for which he yearned.

Subtly, the emphasis of his followers also changed. At one time they would clamour around him for the rods to identify their allergies and the possible source of their aches and pains, but now they pressed him to tell them how much 'alien' DNA they carried. He would give them an answer as a percentage of their overall DNA. As an engineer, rather than a scientist, Bob had little idea of what this actually meant. He had no real understanding of the difference between DNA, RNA, genes or chromosomes; he was merely reporting the answers to the questions given to the rods. In this case, the results could not be influenced by pre-knowledge or expectation as there was none. Most people were reported to have about 10% of alien DNA although it did vary slightly between individuals. One extra-ordinary young man, who admitted to having regular violent dreams, out-of-body experiences and seeing visions, registered a staggering 48%. All this was very strange and inexplicable at the time.

It was three years after the final 'spectacular happening' of this tale when the writing was almost finished, that some possible light was shed on this phenomenon. The scribe came across Sam Kean's book 'The Violinist's Thumb' written in 2012. It is a fascinating journey of our genetic development from primordial times, indicating dislocations in the steady development of the human species and details the various paths research took to our present knowledge of the Human Genome. The part that may be relevant to our findings here, concerns a quirk or kink in the regular pattern, is covered in the book under a sub-heading, "How much of our DNA is actually human?"

The research leading up to the discovery began as early as 1909 when it was shown by Peyton Rous that malignant tumours could be passed from one chicken to another in the absence of tumour cells. A mash of tumour cells was filtered to remove the cells and the fluid remaining was injected into a second chicken. This chicken developed a cancer. Even when the fluid was injected across different strains it always produced a tumour. Rous determined that it was a virus that was producing the cancer. Although at the time his research was scorned and over the next few decades gradually forgotten, by the 1950s scientists had determined that some cancer cells are the result of a genetic malfunction and started looking for the cause of this. The possible influence of viral activity, in this development of cells, re-awakened vague memories of Peyton's hens.

However, while not all viruses cause disease, their behaviour is insidious, and scientists were soon looking more closely at the genetic structure of the viruses themselves. Although not technically alive, viruses use their genetic material to infiltrate cells and make copies of themselves.

By the 1970s Crick and Watson had established the structure of DNA and the behaviour of DNA had become a primary topic for research.

The 2000 Human Genome project recorded that certain viruses can manipulate DNA and can also mask their own DNA to evade the host body's defence mechanisms, infiltrating the cell and integrating with the human DNA. It soon became obvious that the very name

Human Genome Project was itself a misnomer, because it turned out that about 8% of our genome isn't human at all; "a quarter of a billion of our base pairs are old virus genes". The scientist Robin Weiss commented "If Charles Darwin re-appeared today, he might be surprised to learn that humans descended from viruses as well as from apes." (Ref: 'The Violinist's Thumb'.)

Viruses can also infiltrate sperm or egg cells and trick the host into passing on viral genes to the next generation, allowing the virus to live indefinitely.

These viruses have been invading DNA from the start of life. Some are millions of years old. The DNA that is produced by the retrovirus is distinct from human DNA, it has tricked the body's defence system and has not been rejected and yet it is 'alien' to the human genome.

Could this be the 'alien' DNA that the rods are detecting?

While science has confirmed the presence in our cells of DNA that is not part of the human genome and also that this viral intervention has taken place intermittently since primordial life and hence our ancestral DNA was first formed, millions of years ago, it has given us no clear indication of the origin of those 'special' viruses.

It is clear that these viruses are able to modify human DNA and replicate the changes. They have even had attributed a measure of 'control' over the activities of the human DNA. However, science has not yet indicated to what degree they have been responsible for influencing human development and for what purpose.

As there are no definitive scientific answers we are free to speculate. Did these extraordinary viruses self-generate on this planet, and if so why?

Another theory is, that along with other extraneous material, they hitched a ride on a colliding meteorite and, not being 'alive' as such, adapted readily and found an appropriate host in the human cell.

Another more extreme speculation is that they were 'sent' to earth over millions of years by a superior intelligence in the Universe, deliberately to 'control' the development of human beings either just for the fun of it, or for some deeper and more Machiavellian purpose.

In this case the scientific facts are as scary as the speculation and whatever the truth, we are unlikely to have it revealed in our lifetimes.

However, the scientific findings did in some way verify the report of the rods. They had clearly indicated the presence of 'alien' DNA and wherever it comes from we certainly do have it!

Of course, our witch and wizard knew nothing of this while they were innocently pursuing their quest for more understanding of the extra-terrestrial.

(While the scribe was still musing on these mysteries, she heard an interview on CBC radio with the director of the NASA Mars Probe Project, and the driver of the craft. They had lost contact with this probe some 15 years ago but had not given up hope of re-connecting with it. When asked about their very personal commitment to 'waking-up' the probe, they made some very interesting comments. They said they felt it was an integral part of themselves or really of mankind. If we could not travel to another planet then the next best thing was to send a mechanism that represented the level of our technical ability. It could therefore be surmised that if humans can do this and other forms of intelligence do exist in the Universe, then why not them. Even if intelligent extra-terrestrial beings have not actually travelled here, maybe investigating craft have been sent. Perhaps these craft carried, not recognisable beings, but viruses; viruses with DNA that could be absorbed by the genes of homo-sapiens and replicate, duplicate and control development.

"But", in the words of the immortal Tom Lehrer, "I digress".)

Chapter Twenty-Three

– FINDING THE 'GRAIL' –

"When shall we three meet again?"
'Macbeth', William Shakespeare

As a child, Steven, Bob's son, had not been aware of his father's rare ability. It was not until they were visiting his father-in-law's property one summer weekend, when he watched amazed as his father dowsed the field, looking for the source of a pollutant destroying the water in their fish pond.

Just like the father before him, the son had no idea that his experience that day would lead to a future lifetime fascination with dowsing and so many related skills and phenomena.

Over the next few years, he found he was spending more and more time researching the many theories propounded to explain and justify dowsing. He had tried out his own skills with the rods and found that he was easily competent, but for him it was not the practice but the theory that attracted him. Always one to challenge accepted lines of thought, he took to scouring the alternative reports and YouTube presentations. He read extensively the work of Graham Hancock, Lynda Moulton Howe, Erich von Daniken and Dr Carmen Boulter from Calgary University, Dr Steven Greer and many others. He found he was discovering links with ancient archaeological sites and unexplained phenomena. He gathered information about the building of the pyramids and the vastly complex mathematics and astronomy involved, and sought explanations of their significance. He took note of any strange and unexplained archaeological finding all over the world from the earliest times. By 2012, he was sharing his reading material and his opinions with his father over lengthy Skype calls. It was Steven who first mentioned Gobeklitepe to his father. Artefacts of the Egyptians and Sumerians were talked about and how some of these items may have reached non-indigenous continents.

The knowledge of engineering and the artistry and the universality of structures and skills appeared so far beyond the ability of Man at the time some discoveries had been aged, the discussion inevitably led to the possibility of extra-terrestrials, and alien intervention of superior intelligence from another planet or world.

Then, in 2015, he had what he could only describe as an 'out-of-body' experience. Without warning a book appeared in front of him. He felt as if he was watching himself reading that book. He watched, mesmerised, as the pages turned unaided. The sheets were covered with lines of zeros and ones and were headed with what appeared like hieroglyphics. (He has read since, that others have had similar images, and have even managed to decipher the encrypted digital code.)

It was the same year that, while driving his young daughter to school, he was stopped at the traffic lights, when a sudden swift movement high in the sky above him attracted his attention. He saw a dish-shaped craft glinting in the sunlight and approaching at a horrifying speed. Just as he thought it was about to crash to earth, a car hooter behind him brought him back to his own situation and the lights had changed. As he moved off, he just spotted the craft veer off at an impossible speed, and then it disappeared. He could only believe he had witnessed an unexplained flying object, a flying saucer.

He felt very much that this was a year that 'things' were happening to him. While surfing the net he had come across a medallion that was said to raise the wearer's vibrational level, or consciousness. He promptly purchased one and, though not being one to wear jewellery, began wearing it on a regular basis. He found he seemed more attuned to the psychic energy around him. He continued to share his learning and experiences with his father, who, in turn, shared with his willing acolyte tales of the dowsing experiences he had with his witch.

Needless-to-say Steven felt excluded from these adventures and was anxious to participate. When he heard that Susy was to visit his father in Canada he realised that this would be his opportunity to meet her and he made plans for his six-hour drive. Susy had barely unpacked when Steven, disguised as his father's chaperone, arrived with his own medallion fully charged and one as a gift for his father.

At this point it may be relevant to mention that Steven, for some time, had had a mild fixation with frogs. From his reading, he was aware that frogs held a special place in some early cultures. We have already seen the significance of the frog in Mi'kmaq traditions. He found that he was conscious of reference to frogs unusually frequently. Frogs regularly appeared in his dreams. It therefore came as no real surprise that on arriving at his father's home he noticed again the sign on the gate "Froggy Bottom", a name inspired by the multitude of small green frogs that hopped around the land. As he approached the house he saw, for the first time, three attractive green (plastic) bullfrogs sitting on a tree stump playing cards. In the house, generally unadorned with small trinkets, his eye was caught by three little frogs sitting on the kitchen shelf and he really began to question whether he was being sent a message when he sat down to supper and went to sprinkle salt and pepper from a pair of charming frogs.

And so, the coven was complete and with all family responsibilities and other distractions conveniently removed, they were free to indulge in the pursuance of their esoteric arts. Their intentions were quite clear. They planned to share knowledge, experience and techniques and by so doing aimed to increase their own psychic powers and raise each other's vibrational level or psychic consciousness. They were experimenting with the unknown.

They firmly believed that their advanced dowsing experiences had led them to seek evidence of extra-terrestrial life. Just like the search for Christ's goblet, or chalice, from the Last Supper, had become the holy grail for Christians, and the search for gold from base metals, the grail for alchemists, so evidence of extra-terrestrial existence had become their grail.

As the three had earlier studied programmes to help them to 'Unlock the power of the mind. To Perceive the Unseen" and so enable, certainly the witch and the wizard, to Remote View, now they turned to the YouTube reports and lectures of ufologists.

They were familiar with the work of Erich von Daniken, 'Chariot of the Gods' and had for some time followed the lectures of Dr Steven Greer.

Dr Steven Greer, formerly a physician and traumatologist, had retired from medical practice to found the Centre for the Study of Extra-terrestrial Intelligence in 1991. He had studied transcendental meditation and had been known to quote Sufi philosophy in his lectures. His work and experience ranged wide.

Believing that corn circles were messages from extra-terrestrials he travelled to England to an area where the circles were most common. He had studied the patterns of earlier circles and produced digital sound wave representations of them. Choosing a likely site, he set up his team one night, and transmitted his digital message to space, in connection with a powerful laser beam. He recorded an answering transmission and found that this had been translated into a visual and very real corn circle – simple this time, an equilateral triangle with a large and perfect sphere at each apex. In one of his YouTube lectures he plays the recording, shows pictures of the corn circle, and claims that when his findings were published, he received messages of interest from members of the Thatcher Government in power at the time and, also no less a figure, than the Queen. It is generally well known that Prince Philip has always shown a keen interest in all reports of UFOs and extra-terrestrials.

From the early days of his Centre, Dr Greer and his colleagues have held lectures and courses that dealt with the power of individual consciousness. They believe that by producing a deeply meditative state it is possible for individuals, but more powerfully like-minded groups, to communicate with extra-terrestrial crafts, and by willing, or calling them in, produce visual images of them. He takes field-trips out to demonstrate this and on one successful occasion was accompanied by a number of members of the French government.

This, then, was exactly what our trio aimed to do. They each felt that the circumstances were right and that they were never likely to have a better opportunity to fulfil their dream.

The first day together was spent in excited chatter and exchange of ideas. After supper the evening was warm, and the dark night sky was ablaze with stars.

The witch, the wizard and the sorcerer's apprentice relaxed on the loungers, and stared at the heavens. It is an ideal place to 'sky-watch' on a clear night uninterrupted by city light pollution. There is often something to see. Shooting stars are a fairly regular occurrence. As the jet stream gradually oscillates from east to west and back, it is often right above the house, and planes between Europe, Scandinavia and the United States, gaining benefit from this air flow, often fly directly overhead. These can be clearly identified as moving dots of light as they twinkle towards their destination at 35–41000ft. It is not unusual to see the odd satellite pass over and one night, thanks to the warning of a radio ham friend, who had been in contact with the shuttle pilot, a group of dinner guests had been lucky enough to watch the space shuttle detach from the space station and move off separately over the distant horizon. As the shuttle passed overhead the gazers were mystified by the appearance of a comet-like tail behind the craft. They had to wait until the national news broadcast the next day before it was revealed that the haze was caused by the shuttle jettisoning the waste water, taken from the space station, as they could not discharge their own waste for fear of affecting the delicate recording instruments which were placed on the outside of the station.

On this halcyon night, the air was still and cloy, and the three peered silently deep into the Milky Way. The stars winked back at them but there was no movement. They spotted three satellites, easily identifiable, moving swiftly in their prescribed orbits, then, all was still again. Then a strange flash was seen over the trees to the south, like a small explosion which shone then died. All agreed that it could have been a meteorite hitting the edge of the atmosphere and burning up. About twenty minutes later there was a second directly high overhead and then a third and finally a fourth out to the west. As they watched impatiently for a fifth flash they witnessed an unexplainable phenomenon. Bob, who had in his youth flown aircraft, was familiar with the night sky and estimated that what they witnessed took place between 80 and 100 miles above the surface of the earth. (While this height would put the sighting in the thermosphere layer of the atmosphere where satellites can be found, it is higher than the mesosphere layer where meteorites burn up.)

However, all three were convinced that what they each saw was no satellite. Suddenly a brilliant white light was directly overhead. It turned to the south-east and zig-zagged wildly for nearly a minute, then swooping round it turned to the west and moved swiftly in a straight line. As abruptly as it appeared it was gone, and our sky-gazers were left speechless with wonder. They were convinced they had witnessed a scene of great significance, but they had no idea what it was, or if it had any real meaning for them.

The next day they were buzzing with the after-effects of their sighting and the following night sought to repeat their experience. However, they were to be disappointed. While the night was again calm and clear there was an uncanny lack of activity and this time even the winking of the stars seemed to mock them, and they went early to bed.

Knowing that whatever they had seen on the previous night, it was certainly an unidentified flying object, and they were confident that it was of extra-terrestrial origin. They thought, perhaps this was the fulfilment of their energy-raising efforts and decided to have a domestic day. Susy was keen to acquire some crystal terminations and Bob knew a garden centre where she could find them. They planned to visit the centre, which was about 20 miles from home, in the afternoon and travel on to a favourite restaurant for an early supper. Oddly, Steven was having a frog day, which did not mean much except that he was particularly aware of frogs and on their way out, they dropped in at a neighbour's house and there on the kitchen table, unexpectedly, sat a frog.

It was a warm and humid day. The air was heavy with electricity and apprehension. Together in the car, they were quiet and contemplative and subconsciously building psychic energy from each other's presence. They arrived at the garden centre highly energetically charged. It was three in the afternoon and the centre, usually buzzing with customers, was remarkably deserted. They decided to take a walk along the pathways through the delightfully landscaped displays where plants and sculptures decorated the edges of ponds and waterfalls.

They had ambled to the far end of the gardens and had turned to retrace their steps when they stopped dead in their tracks. Moving towards them on the path was the giant figure of a frog. They had each seen it but instantly realised that it was no frog but a man-like being with certain features resembling a frog. It was like nothing any of them had seen before. Certain aspects of the image were to be indelibly printed on their memories while others went totally unobserved. The figure approaching them was approximately six feet tall, with a shock of shoulder-length hair that radiated with a golden sheen. His face was also gold with what could only be a nose projecting downwards from high on the forehead, slanting, penetrating slits of eyes and a tight line which represented a mouth. He was wearing an iridescent green cape. His face had the slight amphibian appearance of a frog. Steve would forever refer to him as 'frog-man'.

(When questioned later each of them independently gave an exact description and not one of them had seen either hands or feet.)

After their initial shock they continued moving forward and the figure glided towards them as if floating across the surface. Steven managed to advise his father, "Don't look at him".

As they drew level each of them received a message, but the mouth did not move, and then he had passed. Again,

Steven managed to hiss to his father "Dad, don't turn around", but Bob had turned, in time to see the figure, by then some distance away, slide into the trees on the side and disappear.

Not unexpectedly, the message they all received was exactly the same. They agreed there was no sound, but the words that were telepathically transmitted to them were, "Have you found what you were looking for?" Steven received it with a Canadian accent, while Bob and Susy clearly noted the English tones.

For some moments they were completely stunned, and it was some time before they felt calm enough to continue on the path and even follow him into the under growth, but he had left no signs. Eventually, still shaking from their experience they were able to enter the building to choose Susy's crystals.

While they were left with many questions, the one thing they were quite certain about was that what they had seen was real and no illusion, but also that it was not human. They described the movement as gliding rather than walking and wondered at the sudden appearance and disappearance, but they vigorously disputed that it might have been a mirage or a hologram.

They were convinced that what they had seen was a being from another world. As they discussed and analysed the experience later they were certain, that from the moment he had appeared they had been controlled by him. They were carrying cameras and yet no-one thought to attempt to record his image. Bob believed he had turned immediately to watch him, and yet, although moving gently he was already some distance away, leaving Bob with the impression that there had been a time lag, but no-one had checked their watches.

While Bob and Susy, independently, later produced paintings to describe him, which proved remarkably similar, subsequent research was unable to identify which group of previously reported aliens he belonged to. They ultimately agreed that in spite of his frog-like features he did not have the frame or scales of a Reptilian, and therefore he was most likely to be of Nordic origin. The telepathic message they received as he passed was also the subject of deep speculation. Why had he not only chosen to appear to them, but also communicate with them, and what did the message mean?

All three were quite convinced that, as a result of their efforts to raise their vibrational levels, they were by then ready to receive the confirmation that they were looking for. The long hours of research, the clues brought to them from their advanced dowsing, and the efforts they had made to prepare themselves, had finally brought them the sign that they had so keenly sought – the evidence that there was extra-terrestrial life among us when it chose to show itself.

It was their personal 'grail' and they felt then that they truly had 'found what they were looking for'.

Chapter Twenty-Four

- POST SCRIPT -

Whether the reader can believe this sighting or not, it is recorded as faithfully as possible, and there was no doubting the genuineness of their belief. They were each severely traumatised by the experience, which they all declared 'life-changing'. It had turned their lives around, had up-ended their perceptions and priorities and certainly it had so profound an effect on the wizard that he vowed he would 'never be the same again'. It was to be the culmination of his life's work, the fulfilment of hope beyond all realistic expectation. Maybe it was because the major part of his life lay behind him, but from that point, ordinary everyday life on this planet became less important and he developed an almost obsessive lust for knowledge of possible life in other worlds. Never a religious man, he became more attuned to the spiritual and more open-minded to the belief structures of others. He became overwhelmed by the vastness of the universe and, in spite of the incredible, exponential strides that scientific discovery has made in the last century, how little we actually know and can prove of our true history, our purpose, and the place we hold in that universe.

While normal dowsing has continued, wells have been found, as have lost items, and further archaeological sites have been explored; people have continued to show their fascination and begged for guidance, but no further extra-terrestrial activity or sightings have been experienced.

However, it is perhaps worthy of note that the year following the sighting two competent dowsers from Cyprus were holidaying at separate times in Nova Scotia and were each taken to the site of the visitation. They were shown the path where the alien appeared but were given no indication of where he entered or left the path or the direction in which he was moving. Each dowser was able, not only to record accurately exactly where he joined the path and left the path, but also to pinpoint precisely where he passed our friends.

So great was the energy foot-print left by ET that two years on, yet another dowser, without any clues, was able to confirm the exact same positions.

Happy dowsing!

BIBLIOGRAPHY

This list in no way represents the volume of reading done to support this book. This not only includes books but numerous newspaper reports, magazine articles, YouTube presentations, blogs and Wikipedia entries, some of which have been referenced in the script, where appropriate.

Rather, it is a suggestion of further reading material which may prove of interest to those whose curiosity in this wide ranging subject has been sparked.

BOOKS
Bird, Christopher 'The Divining Hand'
Cooper, Diana 'Enlightenment through Orbs'
Daniken, Erich von 'Chariot of the Gods'
Kean, Sam 'The Violinist's Thumb'
Miller, Hamish and Broadhurst, Paul 'The Sun and the Serpent'
Oldfield, Harry and Coghill, Roger 'The darkside of the Brain'
Osmanagich, Sam 'Bosnian valley of the Pyramids'

YOUTUBE PRESENTERS
Boulter, Dr Carmen
Greer, Dr Steven
Hancock, Dr Graham
Howe, Lynda Moulton

ACKNOWLEDGEMENTS

The author would like to thank everyone who has participated in bringing this volume into your hands, and also you, the reader, for your support.

The proceeds of the sales will be donated to the 'Tatlisu Neolithic Archaeological Reconstruction Project'.